THE GAY HUSBAND CHECKLIST FOR WOMEN WHO WONDER

BY

BONNIE KAYE, M.Ed.

CCB Publishing
British Columbia, Canada

The Gay Husband Checklist for Women Who Wonder

Copyright © 2008 by Bonnie Kaye, M.Ed.
ISBN-13: 978-0-9810246-2-2
Second Edition

Library and Archives Canada Cataloguing in Publication

Kaye, Bonnie, 1951-
The Gay Husband Checklist for Women Who Wonder / by Bonnie Kaye. – 2nd ed.
Previous title: Is he straight? A checklist for women who wonder.
Also available in electronic format.
ISBN 978-0-9810246-2-2
1. Bisexuality in marriage. 2. Closeted gays--Family relationships.
3. Gay men--Family relationships. 4. Gay men--Relations with
heterosexual women. 5. Marital conflict. 6. Self-help techniques.
I. Title.
HQ1035.K38 2008   306.872   C2008-904282-4

Publisher: CCB Publishing
              British Columbia, Canada
              www.ccbpublishing.com

Dedicated to:

- *My mother, who always believed in me and insisted I write this book,*

- *The man in my life who made me believe in myself,*

- *My family members and friends who encourage me daily,*

- *And the wonderful women who pass through my chatroom who give me strength and love weekly*

Other books by Bonnie Kaye

Doomed Grooms: Gay Husbands of Straight Wives

Man Readers: A Woman's Guide to Dysfunctional Men

Straight Wives: Shattered Lives

How I Made My Husband Gay: Myths About Straight Wives

CONTENTS

INTRODUCTION

A woman enters into a marriage with the hopes, dreams, and plans of a happy and fulfilling life with the man with whom she intends to build a life and family. The central theme surrounding these aspirations is the one of honesty. When the man goes into the marriage with the same goals, but leaves out the honesty piece, the marriage is doomed for both parties and their future children.

Over four million women in this country and millions more throughout the world, unknowingly marry homosexual men only to learn at some point why their marriages are so difficult and problematic. In most cases, these men were aware of their homosexuality before the marriage but were hoping for a "miracle" that would change them. Marriage would be the answer to those ever-present gnawing attractions to men that would mysteriously vanish by wishful thinking. Living the "straight life" could change their impulses towards men because their wives would fulfill their sexual needs.

There's no treachery intended here. Let's be logical. We are living in a society that will never accept homosexuality as "normal." Gay people are openly discriminated against and persecuted. They are looked at as being deviant, distorted, and perverted. Families, friends, and associates often cut them off once the truth is known. Isn't it worth taking the chance to change this if marriage might be the answer?

In these enlightened times, we still find an abundance of ignorance towards homosexuality. Gay people are still killed and brutalized by homophobic mobs. The majority of the straight community still believes that "gay" is a choice that someone makes. But why would anyone consciously choose a lifestyle that is scorned by so many?

For approximately 25% of gay men, heterosexual sex is possible, even though it is not preferable. These men have the most difficult time coming to terms with their homosexuality because they can "perform" with a woman. They want the chance to live the American dream, but instead, in time, it becomes a nightmare. Two of the most difficult situations come into play—living a lie on a daily basis, and forcing yourself to be what you are not and cannot be—namely, *straight.*

The women, who are slapped with the truth at the time when it becomes convenient for their husbands to reveal this information, feel trapped in their own personal "twilight zone." After they learn about their husbands' homosexuality, numerous questions arise with limited resources for finding the answers that make sense.

This book has been written to help straight women and gay men understand the dynamics of their marriages by answering the difficult questions that are so confusing. These are answers based on twenty-five years of counseling tens of thousands of women across this country and other parts of the world who have been in these relationships.

Unfortunately, there is no quick fix to alleviate the pain that each woman suffers, but this book will give insight into how and why this happens. Hopefully, you will find the answers you are looking for that will allow you to move towards a happier future.

CHAPTER 1

MY PERSONAL STORY

On September 17, 1982, my husband, Michael, packed two suitcases and stormed out of our home. His parting words were, "I'll be staying with my family. I'll be back next week to pick up the rest of my things."

I watched him throw the luggage into the car and then pull away without turning back for a final glimpse. For a few minutes, I stared out the window, frozen in time. My mind came to a complete stop, but I was soon jolted by the screams of my three-month-old son, Alex. He sensed the tension that filled our home at that moment.

I picked up the baby, placed a bottle in his mouth, and started rocking him back and forth, cradled in my arms. I was too numb to cry, to talk, or even to whisper. I kept rocking the baby in a mechanical, steady rhythm, and I began to remember.

* * * * *

In the spring of 1978, my life was at its best point ever. At the age of twenty-seven, I was the director of a major political organization headquartered in New York City. My job was challenging and very exciting. During that year, I traveled to fifteen cities around the country, appeared on national and local television programs, and interviewed with dozens of magazines and newspapers. I moved to New York from my home in Philadelphia after a year of exhausting commuting.

My personal life had changed dramatically for the better that year. Nine months earlier, I ended a three-year marriage to my first husband, Brad, who suffered from severe depression and anxiety. It was difficult living with a man who was mentally deteriorating week by week in spite of the forced psychotherapy (at my insistence) and the daily doses of antidepressants.

3

Physically, I temporarily conquered a chronic obesity problem that plagued me since childhood. For the first time as an adult, I looked attractive and felt wonderful about my life. Living in New York had been my dream since childhood, and now I had a chance to live out that dream. My life was almost complete—a great job, wonderful friends, and a nice apartment. The only thing missing was a man.

My attitude about men was typical of other women who grew up in what I refer to as the "Cinderella Era." I was born in 1951 when the social climate expected young women to marry shortly after high school or risk being labeled an "old maid." As a child, I was inspired by the fairy tales with the "happily ever after" endings. I was a gawky, overweight teenager whose ultimate goal was to find a loving man who would fall deeply in love with me and take care of my emotional need of being loved unconditionally.

In my desperate attempts to find this love, I began repeating a pattern of entering into destructive and disastrous relationships. My low self-esteem made me an easy target for men who were the takers in life, not the givers. Even though my first marriage failed, and in spite of other previous bad experiences, I was determined to find my soul mate.

When Michael walked into my office in June of 1978 asking to volunteer some of his time to our organization, I sensed there was something special about him. His charismatic nature, comedic wit, and handsome looks intrigued me. He was six feet tall with a shapely muscular body, long chestnut brown hair, and dark green eyes. There was an air of mystery about him that attracted me even more. I invited him to join me for dinner, and he graciously accepted.

We dined in a popular restaurant on the Lower East Side of New York and exchanged our life stories. Before I realized it, three hours had passed and the restaurant was closing. I apologized for taking up so much of Michael's time, but he said that it was the best evening he could ever remember.

As we parted, Michael promised to meet me at my office the next day after work. I went home thinking only of him. I had a strong premonition that this man would be my future husband. He had all of the qualities that I was looking for in a man—strength, intelligence, warmth, compassion, and humor.

Michael kept his word, and the following evening, appeared at my office. He offered to take me to a movie, but I was in the midst of a major advertising campaign and couldn't spare the time. He stayed in the office, making himself useful by answering telephones and greeting other volunteers. By 11:00 p.m., we called it a night and settled for a late night cup of coffee.

Michael and I started spending our free moments together, and several days later, I began falling in love with him. I had always been a romantic, and I convinced myself that our meeting was more than chance—it was destiny. On an impulse, I agreed to move into Michael's apartment four weeks later.

The idea of marriage came up in our early conversations, and once the words were spoken, it seemed to be the natural course to take. We picked a date three months later in September, and we quickly found a hotel for the affair. In the confusion of the wedding preparations, it was easy to overlook some of Michael's imperfections that were becoming more apparent. There were some inconsistencies about his life that I questioned, but I accepted his explanations, wanting to believe him and not the voice of reason in my head that kept saying, "Be careful."

For instance, shortly after we met, I visited Michael in his office. He was employed as an accountant for a small insurance firm. The mail clerk stopped by to chat with him, but Michael never introduced me. When I asked him why, he explained that the co-worker was gay and had a crush on him. Michael didn't want to hurt the clerk's feelings by telling him we were getting married. I thought this sounded strange, but I also knew that Michael was a compassionate person who cared about other people's feelings. He told me it was nothing to worry about. After all, it was the clerk's problem—he was the gay one, not Michael. I thought this was odd, but shrugged it off.

Over the next few weeks, Michael introduced me to his friends that he had had since childhood. They all seemed excited about our upcoming marriage; however, they unanimously displayed surprise. Several of them commented that they thought Michael would never get married. When I told Michael about these comments, he explained that he had always told his friends he was a "confirmed bachelor" until he met me. When I met the members of his family shortly afterwards, they acted equally surprised, but at the same time, they gave us their blessings.

Michael was a volunteer for a local organization that mentored teenagers who were at risk of dropping out of high school. There were usually four or five of these young men surrounding us who looked at Michael as their personal guru. All of them were from dysfunctional families. Some came from homes without a father, while others had parents who were unstable due to drug and alcohol addiction or mental illness.

Between Michael's job and volunteering three times a week, and my twelve-hour workdays, we had little time to spend alone. There always seemed to be people surrounding us, but I convinced myself that this would change after we were married.

Three weeks before the wedding, my friend Zack called me at work and said it was important to talk to me privately. There was a sound of urgency in his voice, so I arranged to meet him later that morning. Zack told me he had a lengthy conversation with Michael the night before. He came to our apartment not knowing that I was still at work, and Michael invited him in for coffee. From the hour conversation they had, Zack believed Michael was "at least bisexual if not homosexual." As soon as the word "homosexual" was spoken, my stomach tightened and my heart started to palpitate. I angrily told Zack that he was mistaken— there was no way Michael could be gay. We had spent numerous nights together making love. Zack meekly apologized for upsetting me but refused to change his story. I asked him what Michael had said that could possibly make him draw this mistaken conclusion. Zack replied that Michael directly told him that he had gay encounters in the past and claimed there was nothing wrong with it.

I wanted to forget this conversation, but I wondered how Michael could tell this to someone who was like a younger brother to me and a close friend. I called Michael at work and told him I wanted to meet him for dinner that night somewhere quiet because I had something I wanted to discuss with him. He sounded worried and repeatedly asked me what was wrong, but I assured him that it was nothing important. I tried to hide the anger in my voice, but he instinctively knew that I was upset. I didn't want to forewarn Michael because I needed to see his facial expressions when I questioned him about his "confessions" to Zack.

Later that evening, we sat down to order dinner with the usual pleasantries, but now forced on my part. After ordering, I told Michael about my conversation with Zack and asked him for an explanation. His face became red and twisted with anger. He was so infuriated that I was afraid he would knock the table over. As I calmed him down, I told him that I wasn't making accusations—I just wanted to know why he would give someone the impression that he was gay.

Michael responded by saying that Zack had started to talk to him about a sexual problem he was having with his girlfriend. Michael could see that Zack was troubled and suspected that the problem might be homosexuality. He didn't want Zack to feel embarrassed, so to ease his discomfort and win his confidence, Michael told Zack that he, too, had engaged in homosexual experiences in the past. He said that he felt bad about "lying," but he wanted Zack to feel that he could relate to his problem. Michael begged me not to repeat this to Zack because it would mean that he betrayed my friend's confidence.

Even though the story was strange, I eagerly accepted Michael's explanation. I was in love, and my wedding day was only a few weeks away. I was not about to risk losing him because of the sexual problems of my friend, and I dismissed Zack's accusations. When Zack called me the next day, I thanked him and told him not to worry about it—everything was under control. We never discussed the conversation again, and Zack quietly disappeared from our lives.

Of course, once the thought of homosexuality was in my head, it was hard not to think about it, but I kept telling myself that I was being ridiculous. Over the years I had been friendly with a few gay men, and they certainly weren't interested in women or marriage. Michael and I had sexual relations two or three times a week, and although he wasn't an expert lover, he was typical of other men who didn't know everything that pleased a woman. This didn't indicate homosexuality—just inexperience.

Michael showed me pictures of women whom he recently dated, and he also had close women friends. Why would a gay man be involved with women? It didn't add up, so I started to feel better. The fact that there was nothing effeminate about Michael also helped ease my fears. He physically appeared to be a man of strength and was nothing like the weak and fragile images associated with homosexuality. I erased these thoughts from my mind and replaced them with our upcoming marriage.

The wedding day took place three months after we met. We had 150 guests who joined us to celebrate. It was a beautiful event, and I felt hopeful that our future would be as wonderful as the wedding. Neither one of us had the energy to think about anything sexual that evening, but we promised to make up for it the next day.

We left for Florida the next morning for a seven-day honeymoon. I was thrilled to be away from the crowds of people that surrounded both of our lives, but specifically the young men Michael played "Big Brother" to who constantly interrupted our free time together with visits and phone calls. Although Michael's volunteer commitment was officially two evenings a week and Sunday afternoon, some of the guys showed up almost every day. I asked Michael to limit these visits because we needed more private time alone, but he brushed me off by saying that I was "overreacting" or being "too possessive."

Our vacation gave us time to talk and to know each other better. During one of those conversations, Michael said he had done some things in the past that he wasn't proud of, but he did them to survive. I tried to get him to talk about these "things," but he refused. My past was far from unblemished, so I disregarded his confessions and wrote them off to his unstable past. Michael was raised by parents who were not equipped to do so. His mother mentally and verbally berated him by calling him obscene names; his father physically abused him. That's why he claimed to be so devoted to troubled youth—he had been one of them. These stories of abuse made me love Michael even more

8

because when he told them, he seemed so vulnerable reflecting the pain he had grown up with.

Every evening during our week away, we made love before going to bed, no matter how tired we were. Michael kept saying that he wanted this to be a week we'd always remember, at least sexually. Sometimes he made sure that I was satisfied, but other times, he pleased himself only, leaving me frustrated. On those occasions, he consoled me by promising to "make it up to me next time."

I have never been assertive sexually, and it was difficult to discuss my sexual needs. I felt it was humiliating to keep reminding Michael that sex was for two people's pleasure, not just for one. In the beginning, Michael was a willing sex partner, but he made it clear that certain things about sex were unpleasant for him. He believed that a woman could be satisfied strictly by the act of intercourse. After our first few encounters left me frustrated, I cautiously explained my need for other ways of sexual stimulation. Michael became defensive, claiming that every woman he had sex with in the past was satisfied with his lovemaking. To give credibility to my point, I provided him with several popular books on the market about women's sexual needs. He eventually conceded that each woman had different sexual desires when I read him selections to emphasize my point. After my campaign for sexual awareness, Michael tried to accommodate my needs at times, but he made it clear that he was doing it for me even though he didn't enjoy it.

This attitude prevailed throughout our marriage and took most of the pleasure out of having sex. I felt as if our sex life was regulated by the "orgasm bank." When Michael didn't bother to satisfy me, he would always say he "owed me one." This was balanced in his mind by the times he satisfied me, but was unable to reach an orgasm, which meant I "owed him one." His debits always outweighed his credits, but I became tired of complaining and keeping score.

When we returned from Florida, I resigned from my job. The position required ten to twelve hours of work a day and extensive traveling. I didn't want to start the marriage with those kinds of demands on my time. Although I firmly believed a new couple needed quality time alone together, Michael felt differently. His group members invaded our home almost every evening for hours. I tried to be patient and understanding, but I resented it. They made me feel uncomfortable, as though I was intruding in my own home with my own husband. When I told Michael that I wanted him to put an end to this chaos, he yelled at me, stating that I was acting "pushy and possessive." I was constantly reminded that I was his wife—not his boss or mother.

I became depressed. We were living in a suburb of New York, far away from the friends I knew and the city that I loved. We moved there following the wedding because Michael started a new job, and this was a more convenient location. I felt an emptiness in my life when I left my job and friends, and the isolation only intensified the void. Overnight, I went from being a person of semi-celebrity status to the wife of a man I hardly knew. I remember walking in our door one day several weeks after our move and thinking to myself, "How did I get here? Six months ago I didn't know this man and now he is my husband." There were still the constant interruptions in our life, leaving little time to build a relationship.

I aired my view to Michael that a marriage needs time and work if it is to grow and survive. I went through a bitter divorce and knew how difficult marriage could be. Michael strongly disagreed—he believed that as long as two people loved each other, this was enough. I tried to win Michael over to my way of thinking, but he kept verbally beating me down with his tongue-lashings. I usually gave in just to keep the peace.

By the sixth month of marriage, our sex life deteriorated rapidly. I felt as though Michael were making love to me more out of obligation than desire. As the months wore on, the frequency continued to decrease. Our sexual activity was reduced to once or twice a month.

When the pattern of diminishing sex started, I spoke to Michael about it. He replied that we were no longer newlyweds, and that married couples don't have sex all of the time. He suggested that something might be wrong with me—perhaps I was a "nymphomaniac." I snapped back that wanting to make love with my husband two or three times a week did not classify me as a sex maniac, but Michael ignored my words. On several occasions, when I brought up our sex life, he became defensive, saying that his lack of interest was due to various pressures, such as financial problems. At other times, he lashed out at me, claiming that my pushiness was a "turn-off" to him. It was difficult for me to think that wanting to make love with my husband was "pushy," but psychologically, his rejection took its toll on me. By the end of our first year of marriage, I learned to keep the thoughts about sex to myself, not wanting to turn Michael off more than he already was.

Between the lack of privacy in our home and the lack of intimacy in our bedroom, I became more depressed. Michael found quality time for everyone else in his life, from the members of his group to his family. Their problems always became his priorities. When I brought up the idea of marriage counseling, he refused to consider it. He claimed that if there were problems in our marriage, they were my problems. He was content in the marriage and didn't need counseling.

At the end of our first year of marriage, we moved to an apartment closer to the city. The move seemed to do miracles for our marriage. Michael became attentive to me for the first time since our courtship, and I felt that our marriage was becoming solid. Our sex life didn't improve, but I hoped that it would if given some time. "Don't push," I told myself. "It will happen on its own with time." People often commented that the first year of marriage is the most difficult, and I was determined to make our second year a better one.

What really made me optimistic was the news I learned a week before our anniversary—I was pregnant! We were so excited, each for different reasons. Michael's family life had been unstable and having children represented the security and sense of belonging that he wanted. Michael believed a child would be someone who belonged to him. He wanted the chance to give his own child the love and security he missed growing up.

I desperately wanted a child because I thought it would bond our marriage and give Michael the stability he needed. I thought that a baby would change Michael's need for his group and instead allow him to focus his energies on his family.

Two months before the baby's birth, I convinced Michael to move from New York to my hometown of Philadelphia. My family lived there, and I wanted to be near them when the baby arrived. This would be the first grandchild in our family, and I wanted my mother and younger sisters to be able to enjoy the baby. I also knew that a hundred-mile move would end the continuing intrusions we had from Michael's youth group members.

For the next few months, I felt that my decision to get married paid off. Michael treated me with the love and affection that had attracted me to him when we first met. I knew how important the baby was to him because he was willing to uproot his life in New York and move away from all that was important to him. Part of his change in attitude for the better was also the fact that our sex life was non-existent during my pregnancy. I had some early complications, and we both decided not to take a chance of a miscarriage by any sexual stimulation. This took the pressure off Michael. When our daughter, Stephanie, was born in 1980, I felt our family was complete, and I was finally at peace.

Michael was a doting father from the first day. He would rush home after work to feed Stephanie and rock her to sleep in his arms singing lullabies. Michael went to bed early so he could take care of her 6:00 a.m. feedings before going to work. He carried her pictures everywhere and brought home a new toy every day for months.

Unfortunately, my false sense of security diminished as the months went on. Michael was overly gregarious, and within a short time, he became the local pied piper and attracted a small group of local troubled teenagers to mentor. Several of his New York members started coming in on Sunday mornings and stayed for the day, invading our new home. Once again, I started to feel like I was living in a teen-age youth center.

Michael made sure to distance the members of his group from me, forbidding them to tell me anything discussed during their sessions. If I asked them how the meetings went, they made it clear that they were not allowed to give any information to "outsiders." They were polite, but made me feel unwelcome in my own home.

Michael's new group consisted of adolescents in their late teens. They all had certain characteristics in common, such as a lack of self-confidence, unstable family lives, poor grades in school, no concrete future aspirations, and an unwavering state of devotion to Michael. I started to view this group as a mini-cult because Michael was involved in all decision-making in their lives. Even though Michael was an excellent mentor, it didn't seem reasonable for them to be this dependent on their leader.

Some of the member's families were annoyed because they seemed to have lost control over their own children. Michael wasn't fazed by the criticisms. He justified it by stating that the parents were to blame for the problems that were there. He believed he was changing their lives in a positive direction because he was able to give them the care and guidance their parents didn't give them. Part of Michael's success was making these teens feel as though each one was the most important part of Michael's life. He spent hours with each one, individually and in the group, talking about life, philosophy, and future career goals. The only thing he asked for in return was loyalty. Michael made the rules, and anyone who questioned them was immediately dismissed. When Michael dismissed a member of the group, the other members also had to turn their backs on him.

By the time of our second anniversary, our life was more chaotic than ever. Michael started a retail clothing business and used the group members to help him run it. Between the business and his volunteer work, our home was constantly overrun with intruders again. When they weren't there in person, they were on the phone or in our discussions and arguments.

At times when my frustration became overwhelming, I would sob hysterically. Michael became alarmed and the daily visits would temporarily stop. But within a few days, they gradually started again always with some excuse of urgency. Before long, things were back to "abnormal." I was not strong enough to give Michael an ultimatum. During our arguments, he was clear that if I made him choose between his life or our family life, our family life would lose. Michael claimed that he would never allow anyone to control his life or tell him what he could or couldn't do. No one had that right, not even his wife. The fact that his activities controlled my life was no concern to him.

I tried to analyze Michael's need for this adoration by others and concluded that he needed to overcome his own insecurities by elevating himself to a role that people admired and looked up to. I worked to overcompensate in our marriage by giving in to almost every demand, hoping that someday *my* love and acceptance would suffice. I was only kidding myself. On some level, I knew it was a losing battle, but I refused to accept it.

In the later part of our second year of our marriage, a young man, Jimmy, joined Michael's group and became a constant visitor in our home. Even though he was almost 18 years old, he refused to make any decision in his life without consulting Michael. Jimmy scared me because his behavior was typical of the cult mentality. He had a glazed blank look in his eyes, and his speech pattern was monotone and deliberate. Michael was spending more time than usual with Jimmy and laughed at my warnings about his mental state. He bragged that since Jimmy joined the group, he left the delinquent crowd he had been part of and stopped taking drugs. When I pointed out that Jimmy had replaced this with an obsession for Michael, he shrugged it off and told me that I was imagining things. Jimmy gave me a very eerie feeling. There were days I would look out my window and see him standing there just staring. Michael blamed me claiming that I caused this by not allowing him in the house whenever he wanted to visit.

Four months after I started complaining about Jimmy, Michael started acting differently. After several nights of restless sleeping, pacing back and forth, and unresponsive conversation, I asked him what was bothering him. I assured Michael that he could discuss anything with me without my getting upset. He was still reluctant, but finally started to talk.

He told me that I was right about Jimmy and his obsession for Michael. He decided he had to do something because Jimmy had become much too dependent on him. I felt a strong sense of relief that Michael finally saw things from my perspective. I told him that the only logical solution was to ask Jimmy to leave the group. Michael said this was impossible to do. He started to list a number of reasons why, such as his concern that Jimmy would go back to drugs and destroy his life. He then casually threw in that something had happened between them during a "moment of weakness." He kept on talking as if nothing out of the norm had been said, but I no longer heard the words he was speaking. I felt a strange fuzziness in my head as if someone had just hit me with a hard object. After that moment passed, I asked Michael what he meant by a "moment of weakness." He refused to reveal any details, assuring me that it was nothing to get upset about. I asked the question again, but Michael told me that my imagination was playing tricks on me.

I stayed awake that night, trying to understand what was going on. If nothing had actually happened between them, then why was Michael so afraid to break his ties with Jimmy? He did tell me that he was afraid that Jimmy might go to his parents and they could "misinterpret" the story, making it into something that it wasn't. He said that he had to keep seeing Jimmy because this was the only way he had some control over the situation.

I pieced together different incidents that made me uneasy during our marriage and a picture began to form. I remembered Michael's statements about having to survive by doing unmentionable things he wasn't proud of. He always quickly added that he did these acts as a teenager and only for money, so I didn't dwell on it. Several times when we were having financial problems, Michael mentioned that he could earn money quickly by dancing in clubs. When he added that it would be an all-male club, I angrily told him it was out of the question. I assumed or maybe hoped this was what he alluded to in his past that he wasn't proud of, but now I wasn't so sure. Other hints started running through my mind.

When we lived in New York City, we often dined in a restaurant located in the gay section of Greenwich Village. Michael told me he spent a lot of time in this area when he was younger. Once we went to a movie theater in that neighborhood, and we were the only male-female couple there. All of the other patrons were men, and many of them were gay couples openly displaying affection. I felt uncomfortable there, especially when some of them were eyeing Michael up and down. When I expressed my discomfort, Michael said I was paranoid. After all, he was a married man and wore a wedding ring to prove it.

Michael pampered himself and looked into the mirror countless times, admiring his good looks. He often remarked that gay men would tell him how handsome he was, and if a gay man says it, you know it is true because they only complimented good-looking men. I thought this was odd, but I assumed his ego needed constant reassurance, and he was not fussy about the source of compliments.

Michael would throw "gay" into our conversations frequently, whether as a joke, an observation of a stranger, or a mocking imitation of the stereotypical movements of an effeminate male's hands and walk. One day we passed a blond teenage boy riding a bicycle, and Michael explained that in the gay world, the boy would be called a "cutie pie." He was annoyed when different co-workers occasionally asked him if he was gay, and he always let them know that he was a married man with a child. However, I remembered the famous quote about protesting too much. I started to feel that my daughter and I were a shield for his denials when someone made this accusation.

When I thought about all these things combined with my friend Zack's warning before the marriage, I concluded that my husband had homosexual tendencies, and might, in fact, be "bisexual."

The next day, I sat Michael down for a talk and stated that I thought he might be bisexual. I didn't ask him directly because I knew he would lie. After the words were spoken, there was neither confirmation nor denial. I quickly added that I could accept that he had "bisexual tendencies." In fact, if once every six months or so he had to go away for a few hours, and I would never have to find out about it, I could live with the situation. And if, by chance, I did find out, I only hoped it would be with a consenting adult and not a teenager. I had the situation all wrapped up neatly under acceptable terms that I could live with. I became sick to my stomach when I visualized Michael with another man, but I was counting on never finding out if it happened.

I understood very little about homosexuality. If I had known more, I would have realized how ridiculous and unrealistic my terms and conditions were. I should have considered that

Michael's approval of this plan was just a tactic to placate me while giving him the green light to continue cheating on me.

I also demanded that Jimmy be removed from our lives, no matter what the consequences were. It was Michael's word against his, and who would believe an unstable teenager over a married man and father? Michael finally agreed, and I started to feel as if I could still hold the marriage together and survive emotionally. I also thought that my extreme generosity would make Michael love me more.

The next few months were calmer. Michael assured me that Jimmy was gone, and he made a sincere effort to keep the other group members out of our personal life. He moved their sessions out of our home and into the store we rented. This made my life much easier because the group had outgrown our home, and I was forced to leave it whenever the meetings took place. This put added strain on me, and made me feel like an outsider in my own home.

Michael started talking about having another child, claiming that a son would be the fulfillment of his lifetime dream and change his focus. He never explained what he meant by his "focus," but I assumed that he meant he would cut down on the time he spent with his group and his "bisexual thoughts." In my desperate attempts to make my marriage work, I manipulated our limited sexual activity to my most fertile days.

A month before our third anniversary, I conceived, but I had mixed feelings. After the initial excitement wore off, I didn't feel the same sense of joy that I had with my first child. Early in the pregnancy, Michael became involved with someone he hired named John who was 19 years old. When I confronted him with my suspicions, he claimed once again that I was crazy and paranoid. By then, I was familiar with his behavior patterns and knew something was going on between them. When I watched Michael get dressed up and put on expensive cologne when he went out, I knew he was feeling an attraction.

On the evening of our third anniversary, Michael told me that he had to do something important and would be home shortly. I prepared a special dinner that sat warming in the oven until he quietly unlocked the door at 3:00 a.m. I was sitting on the living room couch staring blankly at the walls. I didn't say a word while I listened to his explanation. Michael coldly stated that he was trying to find a place for John to stay because he had been kicked out of his house for doing drugs. Michael had the gall to blame me for his absence on our anniversary because I refused to allow John to stay with us.

Up until this point, I never threw the issue of homosexuality in Michael's face, but now I found myself bringing it up in every argument. I distrusted him so much that I suspected him of doing wrong daily even when he wasn't. I began watching the clock every time he left the house, calculating the minutes until he returned. I searched his pockets when he slept, hoping to find evidence to confirm my suspicions. I became a person totally alien even to myself. The worst part was knowing that I was too weak to do anything even if I did find proof.

What I originally saw as strength in Michael was a misconception. He used his strength to bully me, mentally beating me down through verbal abuse. He robbed me of my self-esteem that took years to build up by berating me privately and publicly. He kept telling me that without him, I could never survive alone, and eventually I started to believe that I was helpless. He criticized me daily, finding fault with my parenting skills, housekeeping, family, and friendships. I began to eat to compensate for my unhappiness, and as I gained weight, he said that my size was the cause of his lack of sexual interest. He repeated over and over that no man would ever love me as much as he did, and without him, I would be condemned to a life of loneliness.

I became a prisoner of my own insecurities. I was afraid to leave my home, fearing Michael would bring someone into my bed. Friends who had known me for years questioned what was happening to me. I told my family and closest friends about the problems, and although they were sympathetic, they didn't really understand the situation or have any answers. Michael did his best to distance me from the people I was closest to at the time by starting fights with me in front of them and making them choose sides. My family and friends stopped coming over and instead met me away from home on those rare occasions when I left the house. Michael strongly warned me that he would leave if he ever found out that I discussed his secret with anyone. This included talking to a marriage counselor, even though I pleaded with him to go with me for help. He also threatened that he would not leave alone—he would take the children and I would never see them. With nowhere to turn and living with constant fear, I was left to deal with our problems alone.

When our son, Alex, was born in June of 1982, we were in a state of financial disaster. Our business was quickly going bankrupt, and there was virtually no cash flow coming in. This put additional strain on our marriage, making each day unbearable. I still had moments when strong feelings of love would surface, but they quickly faded underneath my stronger feelings of resentment and hatred. I also despised myself for being too weak to take any positive action. Michael and I had little communication except when we had to discuss something about the children or the business. Most of our conversations were in the form of an argument.

Our marriage had become one of existence—there was no tenderness, intimacy, laughter, or friendship. Our sex life was non-existent, which was fine with me. There was no way I could be aroused by a man who was making my life a living hell. I started to fantasize about ways to kill Michael because I didn't see any way out of the marriage if he was alive. Although it is easy for others to judge a situation and say "walk away," for the person living it day to day, it is never that simple.

Three months after Alex was born, and two weeks before our fourth anniversary, things came to a head. One evening when Michael went to sleep, I saw his wallet sitting on the kitchen table. There was a lined piece of paper conspicuously sticking out. I removed it. When I opened the paper, I saw it was a letter and my eyes immediately skipped down to the signature, which read, "Love, Jimmy." As I went to the top, I read the words that gave me the proof I'd been waiting for. The letter stated that Jimmy still loved Michael even though he had chosen to stay in the marriage. There were two recent occasions mentioned when the two of them had been together even though Michael swore to me that he had never heard from Jimmy again.

After reading the letter, I ran to the bathroom to vomit. When I finished, I woke Michael up and confronted him with the letter. He became enraged and shouted that I had no business reading his private mail, and he was sick of my invasion of his privacy. I told him that I was not giving in this time. He could no longer continue to lie to me and expect me to accept it. He claimed nothing had happened between him and Jimmy, and their encounters had been only by chance. I wanted to believe him, but I could no longer live in a state of denial.

For the next two weeks, we fought constantly, calling each other terrible names and making terrible accusations. Finally, after one very heated argument, Michael packed his bags and left for New York. The marriage was over.

Michael returned a week later with his suitcases in hand, knocking at the door. He decided "to give me one more chance." By this time, it was too late. During the one week of his absence, my mental strength had returned, and I told him that he was not welcome back. Michael was in shock and didn't believe it. He asked me if I was willing to break up a family for my own selfish reasons, and I said, "Yes, yes, yes!"

CHAPTER 2

QUESTIONS MOST ASKED BY STRAIGHT WIVES ABOUT THEIR GAY HUSBANDS

During the last 25 years, I have counseled over 35,000 women who either are or have been married to gay men. I have compiled a list of the questions that are most commonly asked. After reading the answers, you will gain a better insight into the situation.

Q. What is your definition of a "gay" man?
A. I define a man as gay if he fits into any of these categories:
   a. He is presently engaging in extramarital relations with another male.
   b. He has had sex with a male since his marriage, assuming he had no previous sexual contact with males prior to the marriage.
   c. He was involved in a gay relationship prior to the time of marriage other than an adolescent experimentation.
   d. He has not yet acted on his feelings; however, he is discussing the desire to engage in homosexual behavior.
   e. He is sexually aroused by gay porno or websites.

It is not uncommon for males to experiment sexually with other males at some point in their lives, usually during adolescence. If, however, this need for "experimentation" develops at a later age, it does not necessarily denote homosexuality.

After one homosexual encounter, a male may still be confused about his sexual orientation. Perhaps he was nervous and this inhibited his enjoyment. However, by the second or third time, he should have an idea of whether or not gay sex is gratifying or enjoyable for him. By the fourth or fifth encounter, it is no longer an experiment, but rather a preference.

Married men who suddenly express a desire to try gay sex may have been suppressing their needs until that time. That desire was always present even if it had not been acted on. Those men were hoping that marriage would be the "miracle cure" that would make them "normal," but looking back they admit those feelings of attraction for men were always present.

Q. My husband still has sexual relations with me. Doesn't that make him bisexual, rather than gay?
A. Bisexuality is a controversial issue, and there are numerous definitions of this word. I have yet to meet the man who is truly bisexual in the sense that he does not have a sexual preference.

Just because a gay man has sexual relations with a woman, that in and of itself does not mean that he is bisexual. It means that he can *perform* heterosexual sex. Some men perform out of duty, others out of an emotional need, and still others because they need a sexual release and their wives are handy. These men can complete sex, orgasm (sometimes), and a few even feel satisfied, but they still prefer to have sex with a male partner.

Often, the gay husband and the straight wife use the term "bisexual" because it is easier to deal with emotionally. It is more acceptable in our homophobic society and justifies a reason for keeping a marriage together. It is difficult for both partners to come to terms with homosexuality, and the classification of "bisexual" postpones the inevitable of dealing with the issue. I address the issue of bisexuality in a later chapter in this book.

Q. Why is my husband gay?
A. There are various theories about why a person is gay, but none has been proven completely. Some say genetics, while others say environmental factors. I believe that homosexuality is determined before birth. I have seen families where there are five children and one is gay, or four children and two are gay. If environment is the main factor, why aren't all of the children gay?

Some people say that homosexuality is caused by a domineering mother and a passive father, claiming the father is a poor role model. Others say this occurs in families where the mother is passive and the father is aggressive and a poor role model. Almost everyone has one of these parent combinations, and yet, most of society is not homosexual. Although environment may have some effect, it is unlikely to determine a person's sexual preference.

An example that challenges the environmental theory focuses on men who are in prisons. It is common for men who are straight to participate in gay sex while they are confined for a long period of time with no access to women, even though they had never considered homosexual relations prior to imprisonment. When these men are released from prison, they resume sexual relations with women without giving a thought to returning to gay sex. Even though they actively participated in homosexuality for long periods of time because of environmental factors, their basic sexual instincts did not change.

Q. Didn't my husband know he was gay before he got married?
A. Chances are he did know something was different, but like you, he was misinformed. He thought that as long as he could "perform" with a woman, he was or really could be straight. He may have had one or more gay encounters with little success and/or lots of guilt and concluded that the straight world was where he belonged.

I have met gay men who insisted they didn't know for sure that they were gay until after their marriages. But, even though this discovery came late, these men knew that there was something different about their sexuality, even if they didn't pinpoint their feelings as homosexual.

Q. Why would a person who knows he is gay want to marry?
A. Gay men marry for a variety of reasons. The most common reason is because they are hoping for a miracle "cure" that will make them straight. Gay men who can function sexually with women (approximately 25%) often feel that their sexual desire for men will diminish once they are married and domestically settled. Marriage provides the illusion of heterosexuality, but it is only temporary. Within a short time, the husband realizes that his sexual urges for men are just as strong as ever, and the

excitement he feels for his wife can never compare to the excitement he feels about men.

Other gay men marry because they have been brought up with the same American dream as straight men—the loving wife and the children in the house with the picket fence. For younger men in their twenties and thirties, the gay world often proves frustrating or empty. This results in the American dream looking better and better, causing gay men to convince themselves that they are ready to "give up the gay life and go straight."

Another reason gay men marry is their desire to have children. Though paternal feelings can be genuine, fatherhood also creates a safe family unit and proves one's masculinity to the outside world.

Gay men also marry because marriage provides a cover in today's still homophobic society. Many high-level jobs would not promote a person to a higher level if homosexuality is suspected. Marriage and the family is a perfect cover and it allays the fears of the suspicious.

The ability to sexually function with a woman prompts 20 – 25% of gay men into marriage because in this situation they can cling to the illusion that they are straight. These are the men I feel most sorry for. They are neither here nor there, fish nor fowl, caught in between two worlds, neither of which they feel completely comfortable in. In most cases, they do not find sustained happiness in their lives because of their inability to come to terms with themselves.

I have also met men who deny their homosexuality for years, even though they have regular homosexual encounters. I have questioned these men about how they can deny this side of themselves, but they honestly can't come to terms with it. They need to believe they are straight to such a degree that they deny their gayness altogether.

Q. Since my husband can function sexually in a heterosexual manner why does he "choose" the gay lifestyle?
A. This is a statement that I often hear from straight people—"It's his choice to be gay. He doesn't have to be if he doesn't want to be. After all, he's married (or has been married) and has children!"

When you think about this statement, you'll realize how ridiculous it is. Why would anyone "choose" to be gay? Why would someone consciously choose to be part of a world that is frequently viewed by society as deviant or perverted? Why would anyone risk losing his family, home, job, and reputation if given a choice?

I surveyed 350 gay men and asked all of them the same question: "If you could take a pill tonight that would make you straight by morning, would you take it?" I received a resounding "yes" from 337 of those surveyed. Ten of them were not sure, and three said no. The overwhelming response came not out of shame, but out of a sense of reality. The world has not accepted homosexuality, and the gay lifestyle is not an easy one. How much simpler life would be for these men, if only they were straight.

A person does not "choose" his sexuality any more than he chooses his race or height. Once someone is gay, regardless of how we can dispute how he became gay (nature vs. nurture), that is his orientation. A person can suppress or repress his sexual preference for an indefinite period of time, but eventually, in most cases, learns to come to terms with his true self.

Q. Can my husband's homosexuality be helped through some kind of therapy?
A. *No!* Some men spend years of their lives and waste thousands of dollars looking for a "cure" that does not exist. There are groups such as "Homosexuals Anonymous" and the ex-gay ministries that convince gay men that they can change if their belief in God is strong enough. "Aversion therapy" is a treatment that shows films to gay men that are meant to turn them away from their inborn orientation. These tactics may cause a temporary shift in sexual practices, but they by no means change the person's homosexual desire.

The mind is a powerful tool, and a person can talk himself into another state of mind. However, somewhere down the line, a person's natural orientation will surface.

There are people who insist that God, therapy, or other miracles are the solution. However, I question the quality of life of someone who has to live being something he is not. Is it fair to a person to have to change his personality or orientation just to conform to the rules or beliefs of society? How happy can that person be if he can't be himself and has to be constantly on guard to hide his natural inclinations and feelings?

Gay men who suppress their sexuality to pass in the straight world often become mentally and/or physically abusive to their wives. They blame their wives, their closest and most convenient target, for forcing them to live a lie, even when the wife is clueless to her husband's homosexuality. Obviously, this is no way for a marriage to exist.

Q. My husband claims that he has not acted on his homosexuality for two (five, ten, etc.) years. Is it possible that he is over it?
A. A man does not "get over" his homosexuality. He may be sincere and honest in his belief that he is no longer gay, but the fact remains that a person's sexual orientation does not change.

In an effort to save their marriage, job position, respectability, and family acceptance, some men make a valiant effort to change and repress their sexual desires for an indefinite amount of time. Eventually, those feelings surface, and the problem must be faced again.

Often, gay men who are married will tell their wives, "It's over, I got it out of my system," or "I've outgrown those feelings," or "I was just experimenting," or "It was just a sexual impulse, but now it's over and I'm ready to be a good husband." Although these words may be sincerely meant when spoken, they are not realistic. The wife is so desperate to resolve the problem that she believes and accepts these explanations. Unfortunately, it is just a temporary reprieve. Within time, the pattern will recur, and the wife will be back where she started, with more years wasted on an impossible dream.

Q. My husband insists that if I had been a better (more attractive, more supportive, less demanding, etc.) wife, he would not have turned to someone of the same sex. Is this true?

A. *Absolutely not.* Your husband was gay long before both of you ever met. His conscious attraction for men may not have surfaced until after your marriage, but it was there, either suppressed or denied.

Due to the difficulty of accepting homosexuality within himself, the gay husband will often blame his wife for his sexual orientation. This practice of shifting blame is one of the ways wives of gay men become mentally beaten down and lose their self-esteem. What can be more psychologically damaging than thinking you are responsible for your husband's turning to other men? This head game is usually quite successful because most women don't understand homosexuality. They think that just because their husbands married them and that they had sex that produced children, they are straight.

All of a sudden, it "appears" as if the husband is losing his sexual desire for his wife, as his desire for men is increasing. What the wife doesn't know is that her husband's need for men was always greater than his need for her, and that his sexual desire for his wife was much more emotional than physical.

Ironically, if there is a common personality trait among wives of gay men, it is the fact that they are usually more supportive and understanding while being less demanding than other women. This is what attracts gay men to them—their belief that their wives' accepting personalities will extend to their hidden homosexuality if the truth does get out.

Wives of gay men come in all different shapes, sizes, colors, and nationalities. The average woman who marries a gay man looks the same as the average woman who marries a straight man. Even if the wife looks like Miss America, she can never be attractive enough to change her husband's proclivity. Women simply have the wrong "plumbing," and that's all there is to it!

Q. Why did my husband choose to tell me about his homosexuality at this particular point in our marriage?
A. There is no set time when a man decides to reveal this information to his wife. Some men come out within the first year of marriage, while other men wait until their 25th, 30th, or 40th

wedding anniversary or even later. A husband's decision to come out is usually based on at least one of the following factors:

1. He gets tired of living a lie and coping with the guilt.
2. He has met a man with whom he wants to have a relationship.
3. He is ready to leave the marriage and is strong enough to tell his wife the truth.
4. He has acted on his gay sexual needs and now is finally sure about his sexuality and doesn't want to hide it.
5. He is going through mid-life crisis and changes.
6. He has experienced the death of a close loved one.

In most of the cases that I know, the husband comes out at his convenience, not at the wife's, and this is usually at a time when he doesn't care whether or not his wife will accept his being gay. In most cases, he has met someone and wants to start a relationship with him. Or he becomes mentally and emotionally strong enough to become part of the gay world.

There are women who have told me, "He shouldn't have told me when he did—it wasn't a good time." Let's be honest, could there ever be a good time to hear this news? Of course not. This news is devastating no matter when you hear it. The sooner you learn about your husband's homosexuality, the better it is for you. Think of all of the women who never find out what is wrong in their marriage and go through life thinking there is something wrong with them. Statistics show that nearly 65% of gay married men will never tell the truths to their wives, letting them linger in self-doubt and unhappiness for years. It is better to find out too soon than too late, and no matter when you find out, it isn't soon enough.

Q. I have been told that it was impossible for me not to know that my husband was gay before we were married, and that subconsciously, I must have wanted to marry a gay man. Is this possible?
A. I hear gay men use this reason as an excuse for why it was okay not to inform their wives, but I don't believe this is true overall. In most instances, it is impossible to know ahead of time that a spouse is gay, especially if he is making every effort to hide it. Some women have told me that they were drawn to their

husbands because they were nurturing, caring, and affectionate. They appreciated the fact that their spouse wasn't looking to jump into sexual relations immediately like many men are. Other women had limited experiences with men, and even if they thought something was not quite right, they didn't understand what it could be. Most straight women have very limited experiences with gay men. Why would they think that a gay man would want to or even be able to have a relationship with a straight woman? For the small number of women that I have spoken to who knew that their husbands were gay prior to marriage (approximately 5%), most believed that marriage would change their husband's sexual orientation.

I have spoken to some women who are afraid to get involved in a relationship again because they are convinced that somehow, on a subconscious level, they will be attracted to another gay man. If this starts to become a pattern, it is certainly worth looking into through personal counseling. But most women will be cautious in their approach to dating and have a better idea of what to look for in a partner.

Q. My husband feels that since he can be honest with himself about his sexuality, he'd like to be honest with our children. I am not comfortable with this. How do I handle this?

A. This problem occurs in most families, and the answer is complex. The most important issue to focus on is the welfare of the child or children. Any decision that is made should be thought out with the best interests of the children in mind. Often, children are caught up in the battles of the parents' morals and egos, and they come out the losers.

How your child reacts to this news will depend on several factors:

1. Age—If a child is too young to comprehend the concept of sexuality, it can be damaging to discuss this. If a child is nearing adolescence, it is advisable not to reveal this information. For teenagers, sexuality is such a sensitive issue that this piece of information can definitely confuse the teenager even more. It

causes the child to start questioning his/her own sexuality and feel an added burden.

2. Location of residency—If you live in an area that is very conservative, church-oriented, or far away from a large metropolitan city, chances are that the community will not be too accepting of homosexuality in general. Local attitudes definitely influence the way a child thinks. In large cities where gay communities are more visible and people tend to be more accepting in their attitudes in general, there is a better chance for your child to feel more comfortable about this because chances are the gay father may feel more comfortable.

3. Relationship between father and child—If a father has a close, nurturing relationship with his child(ren), the news will be easier to accept, especially if the father plans to continue the family relationship in the same vein. If the father has been aloof, abusive, uncaring, uncommunicative, etc., his homosexuality is just one more disappointment.

4. Relationship between the parents:

(a) If living together—If both parties have come to terms with this situation and decided to deal with it as best as they can, fighting and hostilities should be at a minimum. But if either partner resents being in the marriage and conflicts are a common event, the child will blame homosexuality for the unrest in his/her home.

(b) If living apart—I always say that when children are involved, you are tied together for life, so it is preferable to be friends than enemies for the sake of the children. If both parents have an understanding of each other's values and put the welfare of the child before personal desires, pleasures, or judgments, the child will have an easier time accepting the gay parent. If the straight mother condemns, downgrades, criticizes, ridicules or calls the father names, it will be difficult for the child to have positive feelings about the gay parent.

Much of this depends on the next issue:

5. How the gay father handles his sexuality—I do not feel there is any reason for a parent to behave in a way that makes his child uncomfortable. If a child cannot deal with the father's homosexuality, then he/she should not be exposed to the father's

gay lover(s), organizations, or hangouts. Homosexuality may be a lifestyle, but it is one that does not have to be displayed publicly. Fathers who constantly shove their homosexuality at their children are not helping them accept the situation, but rather turning them off even more.

It is important for the child to be given the time he/she needs to adjust to this situation while at the same time, to receive positive reinforcement from both parents. If a child does not accept the situation, the father should not take the attitude of, "Well, the hell with him/her, it's my life and I'll do what I want. After all, he's/she's only a kid." That attitude will hinder any chance for a positive father-child relationship. The father should send the child cards or letters that reassure his love and availability. When a child does start spending time with his father again, the father should do everything possible to make sure that it is quality father/child time—not father, child and lover or other friends. Be aware of the child's needs. Remember, it took the father a long time to accept his own homosexuality; the child may also need a long period of time to deal with it.

Q. If my husband is gay, is there any greater chance that my child or children will be gay?
A. This is a difficult question to answer because there is not enough scientific information on this. Statistically, it is said that 10% of the general population is gay. From several limited studies that I have seen over the years, statistics state that the number of children born gay with one gay parent is between 10% and 18%. It is not unusual for children of gay parents to question their sexuality more frequently than other children. Whether or not this is cause for concern has not been scientifically researched enough to make any concrete conclusions. However, if you believe the theory as I do about homosexuality being genetic, it would only follow that the chances of having a gay child are definitely higher.

Q. In desperately trying to keep my marriage together, I have tried to be open minded by reading books about homo-sexuality, going to gay bars, and going to meetings with other

couples in the same situation. **After a year of trying to relate, I am less comfortable than ever and thinking of divorce. Do you think I need more time to adjust or that I am not open minded enough?**

A. It is not uncommon for some women to do everything possible to try to understand their husbands' homosexual world, including being part of it. During the first year that I started my support group, I spent a significant amount of time learning about the gay community. I felt it was unfair to talk about gay issues unless I understood what they were really about.

After a year of "relating," I removed myself from the gay scene because I found myself getting depressed. I was constantly reminded of the horrors of my own marriage, and I kept reliving parts of my nightmare every time I went into a gay club or meeting. Although I did gain a valuable education about gay lifestyles, mentalities, and values, my advice to women who think that joining in on their husbands' lifestyle may help their marriage is: *don't do it!*

The more time you spend in this world that is not yours, the more confused, depressed, and demoralized you will become. There is nothing wrong with feeling uncomfortable about homosexuality—*especially when it is part of your marriage!* No matter how open and accepting we are of others and what they choose to do in their lives, the situation becomes quite different once it is forced onto us and into *our* lives. Homosexuality is a way of life that is acceptable to those who are homosexual, but not for those who are not. Your gay husband has no choice in his homosexuality, but you have even less to say about it.

Even women who find themselves accepting of gay people, and, in fact, have gay friends, are confused by their inability to cope with their husbands' homosexuality. Don't fall into this trap. Accepting a stranger's homosexuality or even a friend's does not have a direct effect on your life. Having a gay husband does. You are suddenly thrust into a world that most of us have grown up to believe is amoral, distorted, and taboo. You now visualize your partner for life wrapped in the arms of another man. Some women cannot picture what goes on past that point, but even this limited image is enough to bring on a feeling of heartbreak and revulsion.

Finding out that a spouse is unfaithful with a woman is difficult enough to deal with under ordinary circumstances. Finding out that your spouse is making love to a man is more than most women can cope with. It is ridiculous to think that there is something wrong with you because you are not comfortable with the gay world. Some husbands will try to make their wives feel guilty by telling them about other wives who are accepting of their husbands' homosexuality, and who, in fact, even accompany their husbands to gay bars and outings. Be aware that this is the exception—not the norm. Some women will take desperate measures to save or hold their marriages or hold onto their husbands.

There are a small percentage of women who claim not to be bothered by their husband's sexuality and even go so far as to state that they can deal with another man, but not another woman. Some gay fathers' or gay husbands' organizations will use these women as propaganda to convince other women that having a gay husband is no big deal. *Don't be misled.* It is a *very big deal,* and a woman with a healthy thinking mind will not stay married to a gay man indefinitely.

Q. I have been divorced from my gay husband for two years and almost all aspects of my life have gotten back to normal except for one—sex. For some reason, I just can't resume sexual relations. I freeze up as soon as I get close to someone. Is this unusual?

A. It is very common for women who have had gay husbands to have sexual hang-ups for short or long periods of time after the marriage. During the marriage, a wife is often faced with feelings of inadequacy because her husband does not want her. The sexual patterns of straight couples are considered "abnormal" by the gay spouse, and he often criticizes his wife's sexual needs and desires. In time, this can have a damaging effect on the wife's self-esteem in the bedroom. Some women are told they are responsible for their husbands' turning to men. This leaves them with a strong sense of sexual inadequacy.

Even though you may be able to intellectually comprehend the situation of marrying a gay man and are dealing with it, emotionally it leaves its scars. One of those scars is usually in the area of sex. If you are having difficulty conquering this problem over a long period of time, it is best to seek counseling with someone who specializes in sexual problems.

Q. Should I be worried about AIDS?
A. Most definitely, as well as numerous other sexually transmitted diseases. It never ceases to amaze me that in this day and age of constant reminders and death tolls, men are still not responsible when it comes to having sex with male partners and then with their wives. Through the years, I have counseled dozens of women who contracted AIDS through their husbands and who eventually died a terrible, painful death. For a number of years in the 1980s when AIDS was an automatic death sentence, there seemed to be less risks taken by gay males. But over the last few years, with the discovery of various life-sustaining drugs, it appears that men are taking chances again because they are under the impression that they can continue to live with medication. I have gay friends who have revealed that they are less careful today than five or ten years ago. The truth is that AIDS is *not* a curable disease and people still die from it. If you have the slightest suspicion that your husband has engaged in homosexual activities, even if he staunchly denies it, be safe and take an HIV test. If there is any doubt in your mind about your husband's sexual orientation, make sure that you use protection if you are continuing to have sexual relations with him. My saddest experiences as a counselor came about over the years were when women would call me to tell me that their husbands had AIDS, that they were dying from AIDS, and now their children were being left as orphans. Early detection of HIV can definitely prolong your life. Ignoring the possibility can result in your untimely death.

Nothing distresses me more than women who suspect their husbands are having gay relationships but continue to have unprotected sex with their husbands. When I question them why they are playing Russian roulette, they tell me it's because they don't want their husbands to feel that they can't be trusted. It's incredible that they are willing to prove their love in such a dangerous way. So many of my women have been diagnosed with herpes, syphilis, and pre-cancerous conditions from their gay husbands' infidelity, and yet, unprotected sex goes on.

CHAPTER 3

THE GAY HUSBAND CHECKLIST

The most frequently asked question from women is if there is any way to detect whether or not their husbands are gay and what are the signs.

Unfortunately, there are no definite ways to tell if a man is gay unless he is either honest with you or you catch him in the act. However, there are certain behavior patterns to watch for that may help you come to your own conclusion.

First, learn to understand homosexuality. Most people are under the misconception that a man who is gay is effeminate and swishy, as is stereotyped in the mass media. Although this is true of some gay men, it certainly is not representative of most gay men, **especially those who marry!** For instance, my lack of understanding this aspect of homosexuality put my mind at rest about my ex-husband, even when others confronted me with their suspicions. He was an excellent athlete, which certainly exemplifies "machoness" at its best; therefore, how could he possibly be gay?

Sexual activity is another area that is often a giveaway. Although some gay men can certainly sexually perform with females, they are usually not over anxious about doing it. Touching a woman's vaginal area turns them off. Performing oral sex on their wives is usually out of the question, while wanting it performed to them is a preference.

If you experience a spiraling decline in sexual activity within the first few years together, it is a warning signal. All marriages have their ups and downs sexually that are caused by financial, emotional, family, and stress related problems. However, once the problems are resolved, the sexual activity picks up. Sexual activity in straight men is a common, normal practice. Even if the romance and passion has gone out of the marriage, the need for sexual release is still there. In straight/gay marriages, the decline continues regardless of the other surrounding circumstances because the husband's need for sex is not with a woman but rather with a man.

In a straight/gay relationship, the woman often finds herself the more sexually aggressive partner. This is because the gay spouse is not particularly interested in having sex. If left up to him, sex is only performed as often as necessary to keep the premise going that he is "normal." This is not to say that a gay man cannot be satisfied or achieve an orgasm from sex with his spouse; however, this is not his preference. His enjoyment is based on emotional needs, not sexual ones.

I have spoken to women who have asked me about behavior patterns that I find to be cause for alarm. This is my checklist:

1. **NORMAL SEXUAL APPETITE**

If your sexual needs fall into the realm of "normal" without excessiveness, but your husband tries to make you think that you are a nymphomaniac, you have a problem. To a gay man, normal sexual practices are definitely excessive. In my marriage, which was typical of others in this situation, my husband demeaned me for being "too pushy or too aggressive" by wanting to make love with him. I didn't have excessive sexual needs, but rather I had the normal needs of most women. I would have been happy to have sexual relations twice a week during the first few years of my marriage, but that was too much for my husband. After our first year of marriage, he "performed" once a month for my benefit and it was very empty sex. As much as he pretended to enjoy being with me, I knew that he didn't.

This made me feel as if I wasn't a worthy lover and took the joy out of it for me as well. No woman wants to feel that she cannot please or satisfy her husband. It makes you feel inadequate and flows over to other parts of your life. And no woman wants to feel as if her husband is doing her a favor by making love to her. It is humiliating and embarrassing.

A gay man will do everything to discourage you when it comes to making love. He will come up with more excuses than women who are accused of doing this to avoid sex. Sexual rejection starts stripping away who you are as a woman, making you feel ashamed to want to be intimate. This is his ultimate plan—to make you stop asking for what is rightfully yours.

2. <u>DECLINE IN SEXUAL ACTIVITY EARLY IN THE MARRIAGE</u>

If you experience a spiraling decline in sexual activity within the first few years together, this is a warning sign. All marriages have their peaks and valleys when it comes to sex. This can be caused for a variety of reasons such as financial hardship, family conflicts, emotional traumas, and stress related problems. However, once the problems are resolved, the sexual activity resumes. Sex for straight men is a common, normal practice satisfying a physical need. Even if the romance and passion has disappeared from the marriage, the need for sexual release is still there. In straight/gay marriages, the decline continues regardless of the circumstances—good or bad! This is because the husband's need for sex is not with a woman, but rather with a man.

The sexual relationship is usually abnormal from the beginning of the relationship in the sense that the frequency is not nearly as high as a heterosexual relationship. But the gay male will try harder in the beginning due to the fear of the female questioning of his sexuality. I remember on our honeymoon how my gay husband insisted that we have sex each day, which was out of character with our usual twice a week at that point. He stated that he wanted me to always remember how wonderful our honeymoon was. He used this as a weapon against me in future arguments to convince me that he was perfectly "normal" sexually—after all, we made love every day on our honeymoon. This was his way of letting me know that if there were sexual problems in the marriage, they were due to my inadequacies, not his.

Talking about the word "honeymoon," you need to be aware of the possibility of a tactic that can throw you off somewhere along the line. It is not uncommon when you confront your husband about your suspicions of his being gay that all of a sudden, he will be all over you once again, making you believe that it was just your imagination running away with you. This is what I call the "second honeymoon" period. Bad news--these honeymoons don't last for long. Sometimes they'll last a few weeks or even a few months. But the "honeymoon revisited phase" is usually over within a short amount of time. You see, after your husband lulls you into a false sense of security once again, he feels he has you back where he wants you and so his "Normal," or shall we say, "Abnormal," patterns creep back slowly, or sometimes quickly. But they always come back. I used to hang on to any false hope that came my way no matter how quickly it whizzed past my eyes.

Why do our gay husbands revisit the honeymoon phase? Quite simple. They fear that you now suspect or know the truth about their homosexuality and they are determined to throw you off track and start doubting yourself. They are not ready to be honest, and so they buy time. They become affectionate, attentive, and start to give you unexpected gifts. They say they are willing to work on their "sexual dysfunction." The claim they will go for marriage counseling, and in some cases, give it a try for a few weeks or months.

And you feel good. You start believing that your suspicion about the worst possible scenario is untrue. And all those little signs that you thought were leading you in that direction were really something else. Maybe it was just a curiosity phase. Maybe your husband was having problems from medications. Maybe he does have some gay tendencies, but maybe that's from an extra chromosome or two that have been misplaced. Maybe he's learned his lesson by realizing that you are going to leave your marriage if you find out that he's doing his thing.

Then you think you are so "stupid" when the second honeymoon is over and reality hits again. Please don't apologize or feel stupid. I was lulled endless times into what I wanted to be a functioning marriage. I grasped for any sign of rebuttal from my husband and swore I could make things better if only he would work with me on it. Yes, I even had a couple of extra sexual encounters that *he* initiated in good faith to prove to me that our marriage would be A-okay. But how long could he fool me? He couldn't even fool himself. He couldn't carry out this lie indefinitely, and within a short time, things reverted to where they were—or shall I say deteriorated back to where they were—when I threw out my suspicions.

3. <u>LACK OF SEXUAL AGRESSIVENESS BY THE HUSBAND</u>

In a straight/gay relationship, the woman often finds herself the sexually aggressive partner. This happens because the gay spouse in not interested in having sex. If left up to him, sex is only performed as often as necessary to keep the premise going that he is "normal." This is not to say that a gay man cannot be satisfied or achieve an orgasm from sex with his straight partner; however, it is not his preference. Clearly, whatever satisfaction a gay man achieves sexually is based on his emotional needs, not his sexual ones.

In all fairness, the majority of gay men love their wives at the time of marriage and are trying their best to make it work. They want to be good husbands and understand that sex is part of the package. They do everything possible to fulfill that part of the marriage, even in a minimal way. But don't underestimate their trying. What may seem like a mediocre to poor performance to a woman is truly a very concerted effort on the part of the gay man.

The best way a woman can understand this is to try to picture herself in a sexual situation with a man who is her best friend but who has absolutely no physical appeal to her. She really loves the man on as a friend, and she may even feel he is attractive, but the chemistry is missing. No doubt, if she had to, she could go through the motions and have a sexual encounter. But how often could she continue doing this, even if she loves the person? How rewarding or fulfilling would she find it if she continued doing this just to make the other person happy?

People argue that numerous heterosexual couples find themselves in the same position after a period of time. When the passion and excitement fade due to monotony, growing apart, financial pressures, or other reasons, the thrill is gone and it's difficult, if not impossible to get those feelings back. But with straight/gay couples, the passion and excitement was never really there, making the woman feel that there is something wrong with her from the beginning. Things only go from bad to worse, never having the chance to experience the wonders of mutually satisfying passion and lovemaking.

4. <u>DISGUST OVER NORMAL SEXUAL FUNCTIONS</u>

If your husband is turned-off by the thought of touching your vaginal area or performing oral sex with you, this could be a sign of a problem. It is not uncommon for a gay man to justify his repulsion of performing perfectly normal heterosexual sex by bragging that all the other women he has been with have never complained about his ability as a lover. This is because he has never had a female partner or certainly limited heterosexual sexual experiences. Clearly, there are straight men who are not interested in performing oral sex with women just as there are straight women who refuse to performing oral sex with men. However, touching a woman's vaginal area does not repulse straight men. Also, straight men are turned on by a woman having an orgasm and will try their best to make this happen. A gay man does not become more sexually aroused by a woman being pleased; therefore, a woman's pleasure is not that important to him.

5. <u>ADMISSION TO PAST GAY ENCOUNTERS</u>

If your husband does confess about past sexual encounters with men—Beware! Men are sexual animals by nature. Maybe there was an innocent encounter ONCE when he was growing up like men bragging about their sizes after coming out of a shower. Maybe some play or touching came into effect. It happens. But that's totally different than having actual gay encounters where you are seeking sexual satisfaction from men. And, if a man is trying this kind of sexual encounter once he reaches adulthood, forget it. The fact that he is even giving you this information ahead of time or during the time of your marriage indicates THIS IS A PROBLEM.

Another big giveaway is a confession to sexual abuse during early childhood or adolescence. When gay men are looking to *excuse* those homosexual urges, they may use the "Abuse Excuse" when discussing the situation. The abuse is usually from an uncle, cousin, or family relative who sexually abused your husband when he was younger. Or their lack of sexual appetite with you can also be attributed to "sexual abuse" by an older female when they were younger, starting them off with a "negative" feeling about sexuality. Although some of these excuses may be factual, the bottom line is the same. He is gay, and that can't change.

6. THE WORD BI-CURIOUS OR BISEXUAL COMES UP IN COVERSATION.

This is definitely a major problem. Many gay men who go with women identify themselves as "Bisexual." What this means is that they are emotionally straight but sexually gay. They emotionally require a woman to be by their side but they prefer a man to be in their bed. See the chapter in this book on Bisexuality. Some men who are caught on the computer on gay websites claim that they are "Bi-curious." In other words, they are getting sexually aroused by men. Sad to say, thinking of being with you just isn't doing it. Also beware of the words, "I tried it, but it's not me." If a man is telling you that he tried it but didn't like it, be aware that he may try it at a later time and LIKE IT. Sometimes early gay experiences with men are emotionally disturbing because these men DO NOT WANT TO BE GAY. But that doesn't mean that they can suppress that side of them for a long period of time. Eventually the need to be with men resurfaces, and your husband will act on it in one way or another.

7. THE WORD "SEX ADDICT" COMES UP IN CONVERSATION

I do believe that sexual addiction is different than gay. But before you breathe a sigh of relief, let me say that it is even worse. Men with sexual addictions want sex in all forms and varieties. Some of them want sex with men, some with men and women, some with men, women, and shemales (transsexuals who have not completed the surgery), and some even with animals. These women get confused because their husbands still have sex with women as well as men. The bottom line is this: Who cares? If a man wants a penis, it's still gay sex. Period. On the other hand, another word that sometimes comes up in **"A-sexual."** These are gay men who use the excuse they don't want to have sex with anyone; however, they are still looking at gay porno on the computer. This is GAY. Forget the "A."

8. GAY PORNO ON THE INTERNET OR MOVIES

If your husband spends time on the Internet viewing gay websites or porno, or if he watches gay porno at home, you have reason to be concerned. Sexual pornography arouses straight people, so the watching of porn is not the issue. However, straight men do not watch gay male pornography. Honest. If within a movie there is one scene out of many, fine, but if the scenes are geared in this direction, watch out! Straight men are not stimulated by gay male sex. Two females having sexual activity or even two males having sexual activity with one female may arouse them. But two men--no way!

I have worked with several thousand women whose husbands were obsessed with the Internet. They would spend hours each day closed behind a door looking at material or sending out emails to other men. They would post pictures of themselves on the gay Internet dating services. And, I helped many women uncover this by helping them check where their husbands were going on the Internet.

What's truly amazing is the barrage of lies gay husbands will come up with when you confront them on these things. Some of their responses include:

1. **"I have no idea how they got there. Someone else must have been using the computer."**

   In other words, there are gay men sneaking into your home and using your computer to go to gay pornographic websites right under your nose but you don't notice it.

2. **"A friend of mine at work is having sexual identity problems. He asked me to do some research for him because he's too embarrassed to do it himself or he doesn't have a computer to do research."** This means that your husband must be an exceptional man if he is willing to help a gay man come to terms with his homosexuality by visiting numerous gay porno sites. Does this educate your husband so he can be an effective helper?

3. **"It is normal for men to look at all kinds of sexual sites. It doesn't mean anything just because the sites are gay. It's normal curiosity."** I still haven't met the

straight man yet who is sexually turned on by the site of men having sex. Curiosity may account for a one-time look, but not repeated visits.

4. **"Just because I am looking at gay sites doesn't mean that I am going to have sex with men."** So why isn't he looking at sites with women or where women are having sex with men? Why doesn't that turn him on instead?" And if a man is turned on by watching a penis, are you comfortable with this as his wife? I don't think so.

Don't be fooled by the most foolish of explanations. Gay websites don't mysteriously creep up on your computer's history or temporary Internet files. If you need help in checking these files, just email me for simple step-by-step directions. You can find them under the menu choice of "Catch Him" on my website at **www.Gayhusbands.com.**

One more note—there are some gay men who are very aroused by straight pornography as well which really throws off some women. I have had a few gay men tell me that they prefer watching straight pornography because they fantasize about the men and envision themselves as the woman in the movie. This is not the norm for gay men, but it is for some.

9. GAY FRIENDS

If your mate's closest friend(s) is gay, this indicates a problem. The gay world is entirely different than the straight one, and even though straight people do have gay friends, it is rare for a straight man to have a close friendship with a gay man. If there is more than one close gay friend, you should be concerned. Some straight men have a gay friend because they grew up with the person or they have are co-workers with a gay male, but that is usually the limit. Most straight men feel threatened by the companionship of a gay male friend and worry whether he will make sexual advances. I would like to say that these fears are unfounded, but in some cases that fear does become a reality. Gay men do not have to feel attracted to a man to have sexual relations with him.

10. <u>GAY BARS</u>

A straight man who visits gay bars is definitely suspect. A straight man may go to a gay bar once with a group of friends as a curiosity seeker, but not after that. Straight men are open targets for propositions by gay men for sexual encounters, and this makes them feel extremely uncomfortable. In a gay bar, men are often uninhibited with their sexual gestures. You commonly see men hugging, embracing, kissing, feeling, grinding each other and more because they are in a non-threatening environment where they can be themselves. A straight man is repulsed by a gay bar because of the openness of male sexuality.

11. <u>HOMOPHOBIC COMMENTS</u>

If you find your husband makes out of proportion comments about gay people, gay bars, gay sex, etc., even in a *critical* way, you may have a problem. Gay men in hiding will often mock and imitate other gay men to throw you off-guard and to deflect your suspicions. Some gay men are self-hating and/or homophobic and will criticize homosexuals because they can't come to terms with their own homosexuality.

12. <u>EGO BUILDING BY GAY MEN</u>

If your husband brags about gay men complimenting him on his looks or body and finds it flattering, this is a problem. Straight men are not flattered when other men compliment them. Also, where is he hanging out that often to have more than one gay man compliment him?

* * * * *

One or more of these categories should at least alert you to the fact that there is a problem. The most important factor in any relationship is the amount of time that you have to get to know a person. You are more likely to discover someone's habits a year or two into the relationships than in the beginning when it is easy to impress and mislead someone who has stars in her eyes. If you have any cause for suspicion, hold off from making long-term commitments or getting further involved if you are already committed. For instance, if you are planning on children but have any doubts, hold off. Or if you are supposed to relocate to a new city, delay the move. A gay husband may want his wife to move to a new area away from her family and friends. This takes the wife away from her support system and isolates her, making her more dependent on her spouse and less vulnerable to suspicions that others may have.

There is one final comment I'd like to make here. For years I believed incorrectly that once gay men got older, they would come to terms with themselves and not re-marry again. I WAS WRONG. Through the years I have seen numerous gay men re-marry straight women because they either (1) refuse to come to terms with their homosexuality, (2) need to lead a "respectable" straight life to the public due to religious or political reasons, (3) enjoy the security of a wife and family while leading a sexual double life outside the marriage.

If you've been married to a gay man, you may find yourself back in that position when moving forward and dating again. That is because there is a prototype of a straight woman that gay men seek, and chances are, YOU ARE ONE OF THEM! You can read about this in the following chapter. Be aware of this when you start dating again and be conscious of the signs to look for.

CHAPTER 4

THE CHECKLIST FOR WOMEN WHO ATTRACT GAY MEN

Women also ask me if there is a prototype that a gay man will look for as his wife. Is there a conscious effort on the part of the gay man to find a specific type of woman that would make an ideal spouse? Absolutely!

These are some of the common characteristics I have found in women who marry gay men:

1. LOW SELF-ESTEEM.

Women who have low self-esteem are easy targets for gay men. Women who have low self-esteem are prey for a variety of undesirable men including those who practice physical, mental, and verbal abuse. And, in a society that rewards people for beauty, business savvy, and intelligence, I would estimate that half of all women find themselves lacking in the department of self-esteem for one reason or another. It's not our fault, but rather the fault of a male-driven society that sets these standards of desirability for women. Even if we spend years achieving extraordinary accomplishments, it can take just one jerk to knock down whatever confidence we have built up.

I used to believe that only women who weren't attractive by society's standards of beauty felt bad about themselves. But I learned over the years that even the most beautiful women can lack feelings of self-worth for other reasons too numerous to discuss here. In my support group, I was amazed by some of women who were model beautiful. They didn't lack in their social lives, but they ended up with gay husbands anyway.

The women I counseled who maintained a higher self-image walked away from these marriages more quickly because they believed they deserved better. The ones with lower self-esteem prior to marriage tried to make them work in every possible way, fearing loneliness and financial disaster. They believed that a husband, even a gay one, is better than no husband.

Women with low self-esteem equate being alone as being a failure. They are willing to suffer more than other women. A straight/gay marriage robs them of their self-worth, and they often feel as if they are unable to cope alone. The longer they remain in the marriage, the more their self-confidence erodes, regardless of how strong it starts out.

Gay men easily recognize this trait in women. Either consciously or unconsciously, they choose them as wives knowing that they can do what they want without fearing a penalty if they are caught. They have faith that their spouse will accept their homosexuality, and they are often correct.

2. LIMITED SEXUAL EXPERIENCES.

If a woman has had a diversified sex life, she is able to tell more easily when there is something wrong sexually in a relationship. She may not realize it's because her lover is gay, but she will know that something is off. Many of the women that I spoke to over the years had either very limited numbers of lovers or no sexual encounters prior to marriage. A gay man knows that he will have a difficult time having heterosexual sex and therefore tries to find a woman who will not be able to compare.

3. ABUSIVE SEXUAL EXPERIENCES.

I have worked with hundreds of women who had abusive sexual relationships in the past and were happy to meet someone who was not looking to create a strong sexual relationship. One of my clients, Marybeth, had been raped repeatedly by her stepfather throughout her adolescence. She dreaded having sex with men because of these terrifying experiences. When Marybeth went to college, she took a psychology course and wrote a term paper on incest. A male classmate, Jules, became aware of Marybeth's topic and immediately gravitated to her. He expressed sincere interest and deep compassion about the topic, sensing that she had been an incest victim. He was gay and assumed that she had sexual hang-ups due to her earlier experiences. He admitted to me that she seemed like the perfect choice for a relationship. They had a tremendous amount of things in common, including their jobs, school, and leisure activities.   Neither one of them was interested in a sexual relationship. Marybeth did not think that Jules was gay, but rather a wonderful man who appreciated her for who she was—not for what she would put out in the bedroom.

Jules did not reveal his homosexuality to Marybeth during their two-year courtship. They shared moments of intimacy by lying in bed together and holding each other.   Jules was fighting his homosexuality and hoping that the right woman would take away his attraction to men. He had two previous relationships with men that had left him feeling "dirty." He suppressed his sexual needs throughout the courtship with Marybeth by resorting to masturbation when he had the need. He told Marybeth that he believed that couples should wait to have sex until they were married, and she was flattered and accepted this explanation.

When they did get married, Jules admitted that he was having some concerns about what would happen next sexually. He loved Marybeth very much, but had trouble having or keeping an erection with her. On their honeymoon, he attempted to perform intercourse, but he was just not capable.   Marybeth was not disappointed because she was still overshadowed by her previous abuse problem. She was content with the holding and fondling that both of them were able to do. Ironically, Jules revealed to Marybeth that an uncle had sexually abused him while he was growing up. She transposed her own horrors to him and assumed that was why he had sexual trouble.

Sex never became a major issue to either one during their first year of marriage. They looked for ways to fulfill whatever sexual needs they had, including fondling and touching each other until they reached an orgasm. Jules always felt guilty that he was not able to sexually penetrate Marybeth, but she was still so mentally broken down from her repeated raping that she didn't care. She could have lived this way indefinitely, but Jules couldn't.

One day, he met Carl at work, and there was an instant mutual physical attraction. Jules always wore his wedding band to serve as a deterrent to anyone who might have a sexual interest in him. Carl ignored the ring. When Carl would make sexual innuendoes in conversation, Jules laughed them off at first. After a few months, he wasn't laughing anymore. Carl knew Jules was gay from the first day they met. It was a gut feeling—there were no "tell-tale" signs. Maybe it was a glance that lasted too long or the overly close friendship that developed. By the time Jules and Marybeth celebrated their first wedding anniversary, Jules was sexually involved with Carl.

At first Marybeth didn't know. Jules started to bring Carl home for dinner or to hang out, and Marybeth enjoyed his company. She was glad that Jules had a friend because he didn't have a life outside of her. The trio would go shopping, watch movies, and roam the flea markets together. Carl genuinely liked Marybeth and enjoyed her company. The fact that he was having sex with her husband did not faze him at all.

Marybeth even tried to match Carl up with women, including her younger sister. Carl was not about to reveal his secret to Marybeth and ruin the relationship.

As time went on, Marybeth noticed signs that caused her to think that there might be more than just a friendship between the two men. She quickly dismissed these suspicions, feeling guilty, as if she was betraying Jules. She started observing the interaction between the two men and on a few occasions, noticed little slips. These included too much touching and glances that lasted too long for normal eye contact. Eventually she started to feel like she was the intruder on their relationship. Her observations kicked in too late. By now, Jules was madly in love with Carl, and he was more concerned with Carl's feelings than Marybeth's.

Once Marybeth jokingly made a remark suggesting that something more than friendship was developing between the two men, but Jules reacted with anger. He later admitted that he did that purposely because he wasn't ready to tell the truth. He also knew that Marybeth would feel better if she heard his denials. Even though his wife accepted his sexual limitations, Jules didn't think she would continue to be accepting if she knew he was having relations with someone else.

Jules tried to juggle all ends. Carl was pressuring him to leave Marybeth and move in with him. He tried all kinds of tactics including sex deprivation, talk about his next lover, and even threats to tell Marybeth the truth.

While all of this was going on, Jules was miserable and taking it out on Marybeth. He loved her more than anyone he had loved in his life, but he wasn't in love with her and never could be. He didn't have the same feelings of excitement and passion that he felt for Carl. Jules didn't want to hurt Marybeth, but he was unhappy and blaming her for his unhappiness.

Marybeth knew something was wrong when Carl suddenly stopped coming around. Jules covered up by saying that Carl was busy with a new love interest, but Marybeth didn't understand why they weren't a foursome. Why wouldn't Carl introduce his best friends to his new girlfriend? Jules never responded, but rather changed the subject.

Finally, Jules was on the verge of a nervous breakdown. He felt ripped in half and could no longer cope with his personal agony. He went to Marybeth and held her while he cried hysterically. He begged for her understanding and forgiveness because he could no longer live with the deceit. He blurted out that he and Carl were in a relationship for over a year. He continued that Marybeth was his life, but Carl was his heart. He had to accept that he was gay and didn't want to keep living a lie with someone he loved so much. He explained his doubts about his sexuality since childhood, but hoped that marriage would make the attraction to men disappear. He prayed that his love for Marybeth would take away his gay desires.

They both cried and Marybeth felt totally numb. On one level she was not surprised or shocked. This was her first relationship and she didn't know what to expect. She believed that Jules was her male counterpart. Since she was complacent with limited sexual activity, there was nothing odd about another incest survivor being complacent. Homosexuality never crossed her mind until the friendship with Carl.

Postscript—Marybeth told Jules that she could accept his homosexuality as long as she didn't see him with a lover. Jules was overwhelmed by her generosity. Carl wasn't. He wanted a total relationship and forced Jules to choose. Jules left Marybeth and moved in with Carl.

Eventually Marybeth worked with a therapist who specialized in incest victims and was able to move past her sexual fears. She met a wonderful man and remarried. Today she has two children and a loving relationship with her husband. Jules died in 1993 from AIDS. Carl was not infected with the virus and stayed loyally by his side until his death. Jules and Carl had a turbulent relationship, which was not monogamous; however, they remained living together. At the funeral, Marybeth and Carl made their peace.

4. TOLERANCE AND ACCEPTANCE.

Some wives of gay men are the most tolerant and accepting people that I have ever known. They would be my choice as friends because they have a great sense of humanity. A gay man is attracted to this type of woman because he believes that if the news should come out, the wife will accept the situation because she is so accepting of people in general. These women are different than the ones with low self-esteem. They are generous in their compassion for their gay husbands in their quests for coming to terms with homosexuality, but ultimately, they cannot accept a gay husband. These women have an easier time leaving than the wives who have low self-esteem, and they are often able to build solid friendships with their ex-husbands.

5. UNINFORMED WOMEN.

Ignorance is the best line of strategy for a gay man who wants a wife. I have spoken to thousands of women throughout this country who couldn't understand the concept of having a gay husband. Living in a big city where there is a large gay population is quite different than in a small town where the entire population wouldn't be enough to fill a gay bar. Gay communities, gay bars, and gay organizations don't exist in these towns. Anyone openly gay would be subjected to physical violence and ridicule.

Discovering your husband is gay is a shock to women who live in large cosmopolitan areas where people have been exposed to homosexuality. Imagine how much more disturbing it is for women from small towns who have no understanding because they have never knowingly met anyone who is gay. A gay man can easily hide his sexuality from a woman living under these circumstances.

6. <u>WOMEN SEEKING GAY HUSBANDS</u>.

Lest anyone should misunderstand this concept, let me be very clear. A minute percentage of women are aware that their husbands are gay at the time of the marriage. I find it difficult to believe that any woman would knowingly marry a gay man, but it does happen. From the small number of women I counseled who did, I cannot come up with a generalized profile because each one's reasons are different. The saddest story I heard was from a woman who attended one of my face-to-face support meetings.

Catherine, 26, was a large-boned, overweight female with mousy brown hair hanging over her face, skin scarred from acne, and chipped teeth. She brought Brett, her husband of two years, to the meeting. Brett was a double for Brad Pitt. He had a blonde hair, blue eyes, perfect white teeth, and an athletic body. I felt uncomfortable on the night of their visit because the other gay husbands attending the meeting were making passes at him. We had set the ground rules at our first meeting that there was to be no interaction between husbands who were part of the group. I suppose I was naïve, but I had faith in the gay men in our group in those early days!

Catherine met Brett at a gay bar. She admitted that she was "fag hag," a gay terminology for a straight female who hangs out in gay bars. She started visiting the gay bars in her early 20's when a gay male friend invited her to join him for a drink. She immediately felt comfortable, unlike the straight bars where she was always a wallflower. The only time a man ever spoke to her in a straight bar was when he was drunk, and it was never an enticing conversation. She enjoyed the company of the gay men who treated her like a sister and routinely went to the bars two or three times a week.

The night Brett walked in a bar, her heart skipped a beat and there was love in her eyes. She (as well as most of the men in the bar) wanted him. Catherine knew that dating a gay man was not the same as having gay friends, but didn't care. She walked over to Brett and started talking, and the two became fast friends. After a few weeks, Catherine revealed her feelings to Brett. She was in love with him and wanted to be part of his life under any terms.

She could accept his lifestyle if he was willing to be in a relationship with her.

Brett cared about Catherine, but his feelings for her were different than her feelings for him. He would never love her in the same way a straight man would love her. But Catherine had never been loved by a straight man so this was a moot point. They went out three or four times a week and grew closer the first year. Brett saw beauty within Catherine that no one else had bothered to look for. He was the first and only man who ever took the time to know her as a person. Catherine was obsessively devoted to Brett. She overpowered him with a pure love that he had not found in any male relationship.

After a year, Catherine asked Brett to marry her. She understood that Brett would be dating men and making love to them, and she could accept this as long as he would come home to her. Through the first year of their friendship, Brett was open with Catherine about the men he was seeing and even introduced her to them. Catherine was always cordial, but inside she was hurting. She believed that if they married, someday Brett would give up the gay lifestyle and learn to love her the same way that she loved him. Until that time, she would suffer in silence.

Brett thought it would be "neat" to have a wife and live a gay lifestyle. To him, gay was primarily a sexual state of mind. He hadn't met a man who offered him the family life that Catherine proposed. And Catherine was the best—she knew about his gay sexual relations but never interfered or questioned him. She filled the other voids in his life, so why not have the best of both worlds? He agreed to marry her.

The ceremony took place at the gay bar where they met and all of their friends attended. By that time, Catherine's only friends were the men from the bar. She had no girlfriends and limited contact with her family who lived in the Midwest. When Catherine and Brett came to our meeting, they were looking for acceptance and understanding. They didn't receive it. Our members had difficulty grasping the concept that someone wanted to marry a man knowing up front that he was gay and having sexual relations with other men but not with her. Catherine admitted there was no sex between them, but she retorted that many straight couples stop having sex after a while. Sex was a small part of any relationship—it was the other things that counted.

I think we may have been less judgmental before Catherine made a comment that alienated us. She defensively said, "How would I be able to find such a handsome man who was straight? People look at us wherever we go, and I feel good when other women look at Brett and wish they were me." That said it all for us.

The other women I met who knew about their husbands' homosexuality before marriage had their own set of psychological hang-ups. Some were victims of sexual abuse as children, some had previous physically or emotionally abusive relationships with men, and others were socially unable to connect with straight men. Some of these women never found the companionship with a straight male who cared about them in the way a gay man does on a platonic basis. This led them to falsely hope that their gay friends might change if the circumstances were right. Some believed that they could become personal "messiahs" and rescue these men from an empty life of homosexuality. I was always saddened after meeting these women because I knew that their low self-esteem prior to the marriage would only deteriorate further as the marriage progressed.

7. <u>WOMEN WITH THEIR OWN SEXUAL IDENTITY PROBLEMS</u>.

I have met couples who both came to terms with their homosexuality after they married. The first time I met a twosome like this blew my mind. One spouse not knowing was understandable, but both spouses? As I started meeting other couples in this situation, I began to understand how this happens. Sexuality is such a complex situation, and homosexuality complicates things even more.

I had various responses with this combination. Several of the men said they were attracted to their lesbian mates because there was a sense of boyishness or butch about them that they felt more attracted to than feminine looking women. Others said it was because they were looking for a mate who wasn't sexually aggressive because they were not feeling sexually attracted to women.

Their lesbian mates were also confused about their identities. They were hoping that they could lead a "straight" life even though they had doubts. A man who was not typically macho or sexually aggressive seemed like an ideal candidate. Even though all of the couples I met were aware that something was off about them heterosexually, most had not come to terms with their homosexuality. The majority of the men had experimented sexually with other men before marriage, but did not feel they could fit in the gay world. The majority of women had not experimented with other women prior to marriage, but knew that they had feelings of attraction. All of these couples loved each other on some level prior to marriage, and most of them hoped that marriage would take away their attraction to people of the same sex.

Several of the men admitted they suspected that their wives were lesbians when they met, which was what attracted them to such a relationship. Some of the men were honest about previous homosexual encounters, but added they did not find it fulfilling. This justified their wanting to marry a woman. Several of the wives confided that they felt a sense of relief when they learned this information because they felt their husbands could accept whatever would happen in the future if they actively sought out women.

At least half of these couples had children together. But eventually, the couples that I kept in touch with broke up when they became ready to experience their newly accepted homosexuality. Sometimes it was the man who left, but usually it was the woman when she found the right woman who could offer her what she needed in a relationship. It seemed that women were able to accept their homosexuality easier than the men. Perhaps it's because lesbian women as a rule have more stable relationships than gay men.

CHAPTER 5

HOW AND WHY WOMEN MARRY GAY MEN

Over the years, people on the sidelines have repeatedly asked me this question: "How could you not have known that your husband was gay?" They claim that either on a conscious or unconscious level, I must have known at some point that my husband was gay. I don't agree with their thinking.

My experiences with gay men were typical of the majority of other straight women's, but probably slightly more extensive. When I went to high school in the 1960s, I wasn't aware that I knew anyone who was gay until years afterwards. Three guys I had relationships with during high school came to me at later periods of my life and admitted to me that they were gay. Some of you might think, "Ah hah! Then there was something that drew you to gay men." But I don't believe this is the case at all, and after I explain, I think that you might not only understand, but also wonder about some of your past relationships with certain men.

First, let's review again what most of us believe to be identifiable traits about gay men. It is our understanding that if a man is gay, he is involved sexually with someone else who is a man. This is what makes a man gay. Most people also are under the misconception that if a man is gay, he has stereotypical characteristics that are identified with gay men such as an effeminate walk, a sing-song talk, the limp wrist, a handshake with no grasp, ultra flamboyant clothes, and endless chit-chat about female-oriented topics.

As I stated earlier, I probably had more exposure to gay men than most people had because I lived in Southern California in the late 1960s, where some people were openly and outwardly gay and proud of it. I remember when I first moved to Santa Monica, California at the age of 17, and I met several gay guys who lived on the beach where I hung out. My friends introduced me to a young man, Glen, who was 20 years old. He was six feet three inches tall with wavy dark blonde, shoulder-length hair. He was not particularly handsome, but he had such a charming and charismatic personality. At the time, Glen was at the end of a two-year relationship with a 19-year-old, Larry, whose name he had tattooed inside a big heart on his arm. Larry, like Glen, seemed obviously gay to me. His mannerisms were very effeminate, from the way he walked, to the way he threw back his long brown hair. Larry was also cute and endearing, crying daily because Glen hurt his feelings. These two were not only my visual perception of typical gays, but they also used the lingo of calling Larry "she" or "her" in their conversations. There was a defined role of male and female that each one played.

Glen also had a 40-year-old sugar daddy, Roger, who appeared to be a typical straight businessman. This was the first exposure I knowingly had to a gay man who appeared straight. Roger was a quiet, small-framed man of five feet, four inches, with thinning brown hair and blue eyes. He fell in love with Glen three years earlier when they met at a party. Roger agreed to pay Glen's bills and give him spending money in return for having sex once a week. Roger was also allowed to visit Glen one other day of the week in the chaotic apartment that was always filled with people. Roger had to accept the fact that Glen was with other men, and he had no say as to whom Glen was living or sleeping with. Glen always treated Roger in an embarrassing, humiliating way in front of company, including me. I felt sorry for Roger and after a typical tongue-lashing, asked why he stayed with Glen. He always replied that he was in love and couldn't stand to live without him. Yes, it hurt Roger to see Glen lying in bed with Larry or the barrage of guys that came after Larry, but he had to sit in silence and endure the pain—or else Glen said he would end the relationship.

It was hard for me to believe that Roger was gay from looking or talking to him. He had an excellent job in real estate. He still lived with his mother and never entertained the thought of dating women. He claimed to be a "confirmed bachelor" to anyone who questioned him.

At 17, this all seemed strange to me. I had heard about homosexuals in books, but I never had "officially" or knowingly met any. It seemed to me back then that there was a solution for these "poor, misguided homosexuals." There was nothing that the love of a good woman couldn't cure. I was convinced that if Glen found the right woman, he could turn into the right man. And who would be a better "right woman" for him than me? After two months, I found myself falling in love with Glen and tried to convince him to give me a turn in his life. After all, we were excellent friends, and it would only take a few adjustments to move from a friendship into a relationship.

In retrospect, I suppose that Glen felt he owed it to himself to see if he could be straight. He cared greatly for me as a friend, and we entertained the idea of eloping in Mexico. We even attempted to have sexual relations on three different occasions just to say that we could do it. It was actually amusing trying to have sex with a man who could not keep an erection no matter how hard he tried to fantasize me as a man! I think this is what made us realize we could never work as a couple. I admitted defeat—all of my love could not make this man straight. And it also left a deeply embedded brain message that a gay man could not have straight sex with a woman. This meant I didn't need to worry about future men who might be gay—I'd be able to tell immediately when we got into bed. Right? Well, not exactly. I mentioned earlier the three guys I went with in high school came to terms with their homosexuality in later years. Here is the story of each of them and how their news was revealed.

At the age of 15 in 1966, I was a slightly overweight teenager who didn't fit in among the popular and beautiful. This didn't stop me from flirting or trying to find a boyfriend. The older brother of one of my classmates started talking to me at the bus stop each morning, and before we knew it, we became close friends. Andy was a six foot two inch giant next to my five foot one inch frame. I was always attracted to taller men because they seemed to offer a sense of protection and security to me. He had a ruddy complexion from acne scarring, but other than that, he was handsome with dark brown eyes and hair.

By the summer, Andy and I were an item. His family was vacationing for the summer in Atlantic City, New Jersey, a two-hour bus ride from Philadelphia. Each week, I would sneak on a bus, spend the day with Andy on the beach, come home, and try to figure out how to tell my mother how I got so sunburned!

Unlike other boys I dated that year, Andy made no attempt to do anything physical with me other than hold hands and kiss me goodbye. I was so impressed to find someone who liked and respected me for who I was and not for what I was willing to "put out."

Andy's family was wealthy, and they were unhappy with his choice of a girlfriend. They didn't think that I was from the right social strata for their family and convinced Andy to break up with me by the end of the summer. He was mysteriously whisked out of state to military school with no forwarding address and no information from the family. I was not heartbroken because I was so in love with Andy, but rather because my low self-esteem was knocked a notch lower when Andy's sister told me that his family thought I was not good enough for him.

Nine years later, Andy called me from Miami Beach. He had seen me on a nationally televised show and tracked me back to my office in New York. I was shocked and excited to hear from him. We spoke for a half-hour, and he promised to write me a long letter catching up on the last decade, which I received the following week. He apologized for mysteriously disappearing all those years before, but he explained his parents had made his life unbearable over our relationship. They even threatened not to send him to college if he continued to see me, and he gave in to their demands, never feeling good or right about it.

His letter went on to explain that since that time, he had relocated to Miami Beach and there found the lover he had been searching for. The person's name was David, and they had been living together for two years. He said that he came to terms with being homosexual four years earlier after fighting it all his life.

I wrote back to Andy stating how my heart went out to him and how sorry I felt for his being gay. After all, I knew how difficult being gay could be from my earlier California exposures. Andy was very angry over that statement and wrote back, "Don't feel sorry for me, because I don't feel sorry for myself. I am happy in my life and feel content and fulfilled. I am different than other men, but no less happy."

When I visited Andy several months later, he looked more

handsome than ever, and there certainly was a happier expression on his face than the one I had last seen when we were together. I also noted that his characteristics were much more effeminate than when I had known him. I thought to myself that if I were to meet him now, I could definitely tell he was gay!

When I entered 11th grade, I was best friends with a guy named Richard. He was a year younger than me, and we became inseparable after school hours. Richard was popular with his peers, and several girls had mad crushes on him and would come to me for advice on how to win his favor.

We never thought of each other romantically in the beginning; however, as the months passed, we were spending so much time with each other that we started questioning our feelings for each other. We never fell in love or had the kind of painful feelings that young love brings, but we just felt so good being together.

One night when Richard was visiting me, he brought over a bottle of wine and we began drinking. We were feeling the effects of the alcohol and started holding each other on the couch. One thing led to the next, and before long, we were on the floor, attempting to have sex. Although we went through the motions, there was a sense of emptiness about it. We never completed the act, and I think we both realized that a relationship outside of friendship was not in the cards.

Richard and I remained best friends after this incident. Our sexual moment did not put any distance between us at all. One summer night, two years later, Richard and I went to New York and spent the night in a hotel together. We slept in the same bed, but there was no physical contact at all. We were buddies and happy to remain that way.

Shortly after this, I moved to California for two years, and the next year, Richard went to college in Boston. We stayed in touch by mail for a while, but as he became more acclimated to his new environment, his correspondence lessened. I missed him but was busy with my own life and activities. When Richard called me nearly a year later to tell me that he would be in town and wanted to have dinner, I was thrilled for the opportunity to see him and catch up.

We met at our favorite restaurant in Center City, Philadelphia.

I had just moved back to Philadelphia from California and rented an apartment in the city, so it was a convenient place for both of us to meet. After the customary hugs, kisses, and excitement, we sat down and ordered dinner. While waiting for our food, I chattered on about my life events since our last time together, never thinking that Richard was building up the courage to tell me his news. When I ran out of breath and asked him to tell me everything going on in his life, there was suddenly a strange silence. When I questioned him what was wrong, he said, "There is no easy way to say this, so I'll just say it—I'm gay." Having just returned from California, I didn't seem to be too shocked.

Richard went on to explain that he suspected that he was gay for a number of years, but he couldn't come to terms with it. During our high school days we had a friend named Joey whom everyone assumed was gay because he displayed the stereotypical mannerisms of homosexuality. Richard was so different in his gestures and behavior from Joey that he was sure that he couldn't be the same. Besides, he was adored by so many popular girls in school who wanted to go out with him. He dated a dozen of those girls during high school for different periods of time, and although there were no real commitments, he did seem to have his fair share of fun.

Richard's attraction to men increased during his high school senior year, but he refused to give in to these feelings because he was scared to face the inevitable. He remarked about our weekend trip to New York the summer before he graduated high school. He remembered my remarks about men we passed on the streets whom I found attractive. While I assumed Richard was looking at women, he was really looking at the same men I admired wondering if we had the same taste. He still had not acted on his feelings, but once he started college, that changed.

There was a gay and lesbian support group on campus, and shortly after his arrival, he went there for information. After that, he spent his freshman year exploring his homosexuality and finally came to accept himself for what he was. Ironically, Richard's mannerisms, like Andy's, had changed. I'm not sure whether these mannerisms were purposely hidden or if being with other gay people made them surface. Richard said he finally felt at peace, and although his parents weren't happy about his new lifestyle, they didn't cut him off. In fact, they had allowed him to bring home one of his lovers during a semester break. I think that it was easier for his parents to deal with his homosexuality than what happened to him later in his life.

I will tell you the story of our future meetings because it teaches an important lesson about homosexuality to those people who still believe that people have a choice in their sexuality. Sadly, the overwhelming majority of straight people I talk to today, with all of the information that is available, still believe that sexuality is a choice.

Richard and I lost track of each other after that year. Our lives were both going down different roads, and due to the distance between us, we lost touch. Our paths crossed again eight years later when I lived in New York. I was walking in midtown Manhattan to Macy's department store when a man passed me walking in the opposite direction. We saw each other, but it took us ten seconds to realize the connection. At the same moment, we turned around and ran to each other, simultaneously hugging and crying. After all of our years apart, it was such a shock finding each other in downtown New York. I begged Richard to have a cup of coffee with me, but he seemed uncomfortable with the idea. I couldn't understand his hesitancy and asked him what was wrong. He told me that he had been following my political career, and based on what he had seen, didn't think I would be very understanding about his current activities. I couldn't imagine what they could be. After all, I had no problem dealing with his homosexuality. We had established that years ago. What else could he be referring to? He didn't want to discuss it, but a light went off in my head. He was walking towards the New Yorker Hotel down the block from Macy's, which was occupied by the followers of Reverend Moon. Throughout the mid- and late 1970s, Reverend Moon led the largest cult movement in the country. Thousands of young people from middle and upper class families were selling flowers in airports, train stations, and on the streets to raise the millions of dollars that it took to keep the cult leader living in an elite style. I had met several of these mindless followers who had been alienated from their families and given up their lives to

63

lead the exhausting merry-go-round kind of cult life that Reverend Moon subjected them to. I came out and asked him, "Are you a Moonie?" Richard replied, "Yes."

He went on to explain that he was one of Moon's public relations representatives. The group was publishing a daily national newspaper and Richard was the editor. He also told me that he was getting married the following month in a group wedding with hundreds of other people. I asked how that was possible since he was gay, but he informed me that Reverend Moon had "cured" his homosexuality. Now he was about to embark on a new life with a new wife from Korea.

I guess I was still naïve because even at that point of time I thought that gay people could change—or at least some gay people could change. My proof why I thought this change was possible for some gay people will be told shortly after this story.

I saw Richard two more times after that chance meeting. His cult leaders told him he was not allowed to socialize with me, giving him no choice. All of my attempts to contact him were denied by the switchboard operators at the New Yorker Hotel.

The years passed and I rarely thought about Richard until I saw him on an ABC 20/20 news documentary in 1993. The previews of the program earlier in the week kept advertising life studies of homosexuals who had been "cured." Naturally, I was very interested in seeing this program because by then I knew that there is no "cure" for changing sexuality. In the years after my marriage, I continually read articles about gays who were "cured," circulated by religious organizations which condemned homosexuality. There was publicity about religious groups who ran sessions for gays using aversion therapy in the form of electrical shocks while watching homosexuals together to encourage them not to act on these impulses. These success stories were always being touted for the non-believers like me.

The star of the 20/20 show turned out to be none other than my friend Richard. He was shown with his Korean wife and two young children in a loving family portrait of a happy family. Richard told the story about his homosexual experiences during his late teens and early twenties. He stated that he went for help, without mentioning the source of

the help, and, as a result, he was now "cured and straight." His proof was his wife and children. His story went on for about fifteen minutes and never once mentioned Reverend Moon or his arranged marriage. It infuriated me that millions of Americans were only being given part of a story and not the part that was important. When someone's mind is controlled by outside forces, he can be talked into believing anything, including a change in his sexuality. This kind of story does more harm to gay people than a mob of homophobic crazies because it fuels the minds of sensible, rational people to start thinking like that mob of crazies. It also makes gay people question their own sexuality and sanity while it gives false hopes to those who are looking for a miracle.

The mind is a fragile machine. There are many educated lost souls in this world who are looking for a leader to tell them what to do rather than to trust their own judgment. Even in the 1990s, we have seen examples of cult movements where highly educated people have committed group suicide because they were convinced that their leaders were divine and ordered them to die. I believe this happens more frequently when people are self-hating about what they are. Therefore, I would not be surprised at all to find an out-of-proportion percentage of cult members comprised of people who are confused about their sexuality.

We still live in a society that emphatically tells us that homosexuality is wrong. Gay people are criticized, ridiculed, and often cut off from families and friends. The message is that homosexuality is a choice that people consciously make. Someone who can perform heterosexual sex even if it is not desirable or preferable is compelled to give the "straight life" a chance because in all other respects it is easier.

Richard was such a fun-loving, outwardly happy teenager. When I saw him as an adult under the influence, he was a totally changed person filled with reserve and seriousness. My best friend had disappeared into the will of a stranger who controlled his life.

After this book was first published in 2000, there was a great irony that took place. The same month that my book was being released, Richard Cohen had a book that was being released called "Coming Out Straight." Dr. Laura, the famed media psychologist, wrote the introduction and endorsed the book. I sent out a national press release condemning this, and wrote about it in my newsletter. I wrote:

BONNIE KAYE AND DR. LAURA

*Last month, I received some national publicity for condemning Dr. Laura Schlessinger's endorsement of a book called **"Coming Out Straight"** by Richard Cohen. This is a book that advocates sexual "reorientation" of gay people so they can be straight. Cohen believes that people are born straight, but develop same-sex attractions due to problems in their childhood.*

People wondered why I was surprised at Dr. Laura for endorsing a book that urged gay people to become straight. She is certainly not known for her tolerance of homosexuality. What disturbed me was that Dr. Laura endorsed a book written by a man who was sexually "reoriented" through brainwashing while he was a leader in a cult group led by Rev. Moon. For those of you who are too young to remember this group, it was the largest of cult groups during the 1970's. It ripped families apart by not allowing them near their brainwashed family members. These were the people selling flowers in the streets and airports to raise money to keep their leader in great prosperity. The movement calls itself the "Unification Church." In Cohen's book, he never once mentions Rev. Moon, but he does mention the church on several occasions. Most people confuse that name with the Unitarian Church or make no connection with a cult movement.

The irony of this story is that Richard and I were best friends in high school in the late 1960's. He came to terms with his homosexuality in college, and then became "straight" again after joining the cult group. After a seven-year separation, we ran into each other in 1978 in New York City where we were both about to be married—me unknowingly to a gay husband, and he knowingly to a straight woman. I vividly remember the shock when Richard told me about his upcoming marriage. That's when he explained how Reverend Moon had made him realize that he could be straight and that gay was evil. I was forbidden to see Richard after one more meeting for fear of his being "wrongly influenced." *The next time I heard about Richard was in the early 1990's when he appeared on a 20/20 segment explaining how gay people can become straight. He was shown with his Korean wife and their children as proof of his success. Nowhere in the segment was their any mention of Richard's brainwashing by a cult movement. Even more ironically is how I wrote about Richard in my own book that came out this year—the same month his book came out! I had no idea that Richard was a professional conversion counselor writing a book. Nor did he have any idea that my ex-husband was gay and that I had become a counselor in this field.*

The thinking of Richard Cohen is dangerous. It gives people the impression that gay is a choice that people make due to relationships in their early formative years. It gives people false hope for their futures, and keeps the fires of homophobia burning. It gives a message that our husbands can choose to be straight if they really want to. For those of us living this life, we know this is not true. Even if men can suppress their sexual needs and not act of them, it doesn't mean that they are happy doing this. The frustration that sets in is taken out on the devoted wives who can't understand why they can't make their husbands happy.

Dr. Laura did not do her homework. If she did, I am sure that she would never endorse a former cult leader who was brainwashed into becoming "straight."

My last story begins at the end of my junior year of high school. I started dating a young man, Eric. We met in one of our classes, and from the moment I saw him early in the semester, I couldn't take my eyes off him. He was one of the most handsome guys I had ever seen, standing six feet tall with dark brown hair and eyes. His good looks made him the talk of the girls in school.

He often said hello to me through that year, and on our last day of class, I had the courage to give him my phone number and invite him to get together during the summer if he was available. I never dreamt he would call me, but he did several weeks into June.

Eric invited me to dinner, and I suspected it was because he had an agenda other than dinner. On our first date, we went for Chinese food in a neighborhood restaurant. Afterwards, we went driving in his car and eventually, we ended up at a big make-out place. I waited for his sexual advances to begin, but it didn't happen. We spent the next two hours casually talking and then he took me home. He walked me to the door and gave me an unpassionate goodnight kiss on the lips. I doubted that I would ever hear from him again, but surprisingly, he called several days later and asked me out again.

Over the next few dates, I kept waiting to find us sexually entangled, but it didn't happen. Eric claimed that he found me interesting and fun to be with, and I was under the definite impression he wanted more than friendship. We started talking daily, and he invited me to his home for dinner once a week. I met his parents who were wealthy professionals, and they seemed not to approve of me, much like Andy's parents, but didn't interfere.

After six weeks of steady dating, we finally moved beyond holding hands and kissing. By the end of the summer, we were having sexual relations. It didn't happen every time we were together, but usually once a week. Although I had previous relationships with guys, I was too young and too sexually immature at that age to understand the difference between good and bad sex. I knew we had a problem, but I could never pinpoint it. Eric was moody and sullen at times, which played greatly into my insecurities. I still didn't understand why he was dating me when he could have been dating the most beautiful and popular girls in school. Whenever Eric went into one of his quiet moods, I was sure he was getting ready to break up with me no matter how he assured me that it wasn't my fault.

After nine months of steady dating, I broke up with Eric because I could not deal with his feelings of negativity during his frequent mood swings. Shortly after that, I moved to California and our lives moved in different directions.

I called Eric four years later after the break-up of a two-year live-in relationship. I was feeling depressed about my life and thought perhaps I could recreate a time that seemed happier to me. It's funny how human it is to fantasize a mediocre relationship into a good one when a worse one comes along!

By this time, Eric had just started medical school and invited me to spend the weekend with him in upstate Pennsylvania.

Once there, it seemed as if nothing had changed from several years before—especially in bed. Yes, we had sex, but it seemed very empty and unfulfilling. By now, I had experienced good sex and knew the difference. But okay, I knew sometimes sex could improve over time. Both of us seemed willing to recreate our relationship from high school, but it seemed so forced and difficult. After a few months, we just stopped talking to each other and knew that it was over.

Our paths crossed six years later after the break-up of my first marriage to a straight man. Once again, I thought it was worth a try and tracked Eric down to his new home in Massachusetts. He seemed surprised to hear from me after so much time. I was then living in New York and gave him my phone number, encouraging him to call me when he came into town.

That call came six months later at a time when we were both without partners. When Eric walked into my office, I was thrown off guard. Only six years had passed since our last visit, but he looked like a totally different man. His dress was rather disheveled, he had gained at least thirty pounds, and a portion of his upper hair had fallen out while the remainder looked unkempt. He had never fully recovered from a bout with Bell's Palsy which left one side of his mouth lopsided when he spoke and smiled. I tried to cover my disappointment, but it was difficult. Whatever physical attraction I once had for Eric was gone. I wondered if I could recapture the feelings of excitement that I once had as a love-struck teenager.

Eric took me to dinner in a quiet French restaurant, and then we went back to my apartment where we enjoyed a bottle of wine. We talked through most of the night and he told me about his life since our last time together.

Eric became employed as an oncologist in a Massachusetts hospital two years earlier when he was awarded a fellowship. He bought a single home overlooking a lake, which gave him the peace and solitude he needed in his life. He had met numerous women over the years, especially nurses in the hospitals. He had serious relationships with two of those nurses, but they didn't work out. During that conversation, Eric also mentioned that he had been involved with two men for a short time, but afterwards decided that he was not interested in men. He explained that it was normal for most men to experiment sometime in their lives, and he had done just that.

I was still somewhat naïve about men having these kinds of experiences, but Eric made it sound so natural that I accepted that he experimented twice and realized that he was straight. He gave no indication that he had any further interest in men, but rather stated that it wasn't his "thing."

Our night ended with sex as if we needed to rekindle whatever remnants of the past were left. Once again, it wasn't great. We kissed goodbye with promises to talk and get together soon. After the next few conversations, we decided to give our relationship one more try. Eric always kidded that we were like Barbara Streisand and Robert Redford in the movie, *The Way We Were,* about two college sweethearts that meet up years later and try to rekindle a relationship that never worked to start with.

We met at least two or three times each month. Either Eric would drive to New York or I would fly to Massachusetts to spend long weekends together. This went on for six months, but once again, old patterns returned and my old insecurities resurfaced. I needed verbal reassurance that I was loved and Eric was short on words. They were difficult for him to express, and I felt as if I was always seeking his approval. Even though I had come a long way in my life, I still did not feel worthy of this brilliant man who could have his choice of women but chose to be with me.

Our sex life was out of synch. This is the only way I can describe it. Eric was going through the motions but something was missing. There was no intimacy prior to or following our lovemaking. It was mechanical. I really didn't enjoy it but hoped in time it would improve. He lacked the sense of passion and romance important to me throughout my life.

We were in the planning stages of moving in together when I met Michael, who swept me off my feet. He was fast to fill the void that was missing in my relationship with Eric. Where Eric was cold and detached, Michael was warm and expressive. He was quick to express his feelings of love days into the relationship, which was something that Eric was never able to do.

Eric tracked me down after two weeks of avoiding

communication other than his talking to my answering machine. It was very difficult breaking the news to him that I had met someone else. He couldn't understand how two weeks earlier we were making the same plans to move in together which were now canceled out by a stranger I had just met.

It was difficult explaining this to Eric, and I admitted that I wasn't sure if I was making the right decision. But I also resolved that moving in with him would not have been the right thing either. I felt I had to give my impulsive heart a chance, and I apologized for hurting him once again.

I kept in touch with Eric after I married Michael. He wasn't exactly sure why I kept calling him, and I didn't know myself. I suppose I knew from the beginning that I had made a bad decision when I married Michael and wasn't ready to completely let go of the past. A year after I married Michael, Eric decided to move to New York because he had a prestigious job offer in a local hospital. I helped him find an apartment several blocks away from where I lived. In spite of the close proximity, Eric made it clear that we were not going to be close friends—just casual acquaintances when I needed to talk to him. One time when Michael was feeling very ill, I called Eric for help and he came over. That was the only time Eric and Michael met, and it was awkward for the three of us.

The following year Eric transferred to a hospital in Washington, D.C. I told him I would keep in touch and followed up on that promise every six months. Our conversations were usually strained and short, but I felt compelled to keep in touch with him.

In 1987, several years after my marriage ended and my face-to-face support group dissolved, I called Eric for my biyearly chat. A man answered the phone and told me that Eric was not home. I asked whom I was talking to, and he stated that he was Eric's roommate. For the first time, this eerie feeling came over me. When Eric returned my call, I came right out and asked him if he was gay. He replied, "Yes. How did you know?" By that time, I was so aware of all of the signs that it was obvious to me. Everything finally started to make sense. I now understood why things never totally meshed in our relationship. That conversation was our last conversation.

Some friends advised me not to write this chapter, lest people should think that I am drawn to gay men and have created these tragic situations on my own. I know this is not the case at all. First, let's look at the traits that all of these men had in common to determine if I on some conscious or unconscious level could have known that these men were gay.

All of the men in question, Andy, Richard, Eric, and Michael, were very handsome men. With the exception of Eric, they all had outgoing and friendly personalities. They seemed nurturing, supporting, and respectful of me. None of them seemed to be looking at me as a sex object, which was what most women hope for in their lives. They were all sought after by pretty and popular females. Most importantly, why would I think they were gay?

In the cases of Michael and Eric, both of them performed in bed and reached an orgasm. As I mentioned, it wasn't great sex, but I had worse sex with several other men. In retrospect, they were probably gay, too! I say that now because I have experienced wonderful sexual relationships with straight men, and I know that there is a difference in the way that straight men feel and respond to sex. You can tell that they totally enjoy making love with a woman and want to do anything that will enhance the sexual experience. Now in my forties, I have been most fortunate to find the ultimate love of my life who for over six years has made every sexual experience exciting and fulfilling.

Of the thousands of women I have worked with, a handful claimed that they had sexually satisfying relationships with their gay husbands on a regular basis. These are exceptions to the rule. The rest of the women never had a sexually satisfying relationship or much of a sexual relationship at all. To the credit of some of the gay husbands, they tried their best. They really wanted to satisfy their wives because in most cases, they loved them on some level. But it is impossible to keep living a lie forever, and thus, the sexual part of the relationship deteriorates within a matter of time.

CHAPTER 6

LIVING LA VIDA LIMBO

Let's discuss married gay men who won't leave the marriage or for that matter, won't leave the closet. This is a subject that can never be talked about enough because it seems to be a stumbling block for so many of us who can't get our husbands to "come clean" with the truth about their homosexuality. I receive so many letters each month from women who are sure about their husbands but fear confronting them. But I also get letters from women who do confront their husbands with evidence in hand and get denials with distorted truths giving excuses such as "Those pictures belonged to a co-worker," or "I have no clue how those websites got on our computer."

For those women whose husbands eventually tell you the truth, count yourselves as lucky even though you may not feel that way at the time. No doubt hearing the word *gay* is devastating, but *not* hearing it is even worse. Ask a woman who is trapped in an unfulfilling marriage with a gay man. These women know the truth. They have stumbled on it one way or another. It has smacked them in the face through hidden websites, email, pornography, letters, hotel receipts, phone bills, etc. And yet, their husbands just keep lying or denying. They are not ready to be honest--and may never be ready. Some men will never be ready to accept their homosexuality because it is too painful or embarrassing.

These are the men whom I call the **"Limbo Men."** Their whole lives are lived in limbo. They are emotionally straight, but physically gay. They never feel totally comfortable in either world, but they are much more comfortable "passing" in the straight world where they are accepted as part of mainstream society.

All married gay men go through "limbo" for a period of time. In other words, they are stuck in between both worlds hoping that by wanting the straight world badly enough they will be able to "cross over" into it. They keep thinking that if they play the role long enough, they will become transformed into the part, not just play the part as an actor. But the Limbo Men I place in this category are different from other gay men who eventually come to terms with themselves. They are even different than the gay men who are staying in their marriages but who acknowledge they are gay, at least on some level.

The real Limbo Men have no sense of remorse for what they are doing to their wives. In fact, they often feel as if they are the victims and strike back at their wives in an emotional or physically abusive manner. They blame their wives for their unhappiness and never have a clue about the damage they are doing to these women whom they promised to love, cherish, and respect. They place the blame of their unhappiness on their wives, when in fact, there is nothing that their wives could possibly do to make them feel happy or fulfilled. Their wives are women, and they are gay men.

These are the men who will never leave their marriages. They will stay there until the day they die, leading a painful existence and sharing that pain with their wives. More specifically, pouring that pain upon their wives. We all know that misery loves company, and these men are happy to make you as miserable as they are.

So often, these "Limbo Men" husbands luck out. They have wives who are much kinder and more understanding than average. These are the women who will keep trying every little trick in the book thinking someday they will get their husbands hooked. The women live an accepted existence, looking for the crumbs in the marriage while trying to turn those crumbs into a cake. It is truly a tragedy and waste of human life.

LIMBO WOMEN

Limbo Men create a whole new category of straight wives—namely, **LIMBO WOMEN.** Limbo Women are the wives of Limbo Men who are stuck wasting years of their lives in unsatisfying marriages because they can never quite get the truth out of their husbands. They know that something is wrong. They know that their marriages are lacking the ingredients for success—namely communication, passion, and intimacy. They have loads of little clues that all add up to homosexuality, and yet, because they can't get a full confession—or even a partial confession—they are trapped.

By the time a wife of a Limbo Man gives a confession, it's usually a partial, such as:

1. I'm not gay, but I like looking at gay pornography as part of a full pornographic fantasy show.
2. I'm not gay, but when I was younger, I had an uncle who molested me on a few occasions.
3. I'm not gay, but sometimes I call gay sex lines because the way they talk stimulates me sexually.
4. I'm not gay, but when I was younger, before I met you, I had a one-time sexual encounter with a man, but I only let him perform oral sex on me.
5. I'm not gay, but there are times I think that I am bisexual because I look at guys and find them sexually appealing. I would never act on it though.
6. I'm not gay, but sometimes the thought of anal penetration turns me on.
7. I'm not gay, but when I was in college, we would all get stoned/drunk and have big orgies where everyone was having sex with everyone.
8. I'm not gay, but I have a fantasy about both of us having sex with another man.

The sad part is that each one of these partial confessions always starts the same way: I'M NOT GAY, BUT.... And now the wife is more trapped than ever. How can they break up a marriage just on their own perceptions based on partial truths?

I have wives that write to me about the extensive research they do on human sexuality. They are looking for my stamp of endorsement for their discoveries that their husbands aren't gay, just sexually "different" or "deviant." It seems if they can get my professional opinion that their situation is not like the thousands of others that I have worked with, they can learn to cope in their marriages and accept that life isn't always a bowl of cherries. On the other hand, it's not always a bowl of pits either. It's actually a bowl of half eaten cherries with the pits still in tact—sometimes, anyway.

These women struggle more than those of us who are given our walking papers or as I like to call it, "freedom." Those of us riding the freedom trail may be hurting for a while, but eventually we can lick our wounds and start life over. We don't have the shackles of homosexuality tying us to a husband who just won't be honest with us or in many cases, himself.

Limbo Women have the lowest self-esteem of all of us because they do personalize that the lack of love that their husbands can show them sexually is because of their failings. After they've exhausted every trick known to womankind without any success or movement, they admit defeat. Nothing they do makes it change. No diet, no breast implant, no sexy clothes, no new hair style, no new approaches to sexual satisfaction is going to move their husbands into the straight zone. Eventually, they admit defeat, but still don't understand why everything they try is not working on anything in their relationship.

Some of these wives cope by developing their own "on-the-sides" personal lives. They meet some straight man on the Internet who can boost their self-esteem by telling them all the things their husbands should be saying but don't say. Sometimes these Internet affairs are lifesavers when women start giving up hope on themselves. Some of these wives cope by finding real-life affairs, going outside the boundaries of their morals, religious beliefs, and vows, making them feel better on one end, but worse on the other. And still other women cope by popping pills that numb their minds and lower their libido just so they can keep living in the state of limbo.

And so life just keeps moving along, day-by-day, week-by-week, month-by-month, and year-by-year. Limbo Women attend family holidays, friend events like birthdays and anniversaries, and office Christmas parties of their Limbo Husbands. They stand like a trophy next to a man who needs a wife to show off to prove to the world that **"I AM NOT GAY. HERE IS MY PROOF."** The Limbo Wife *allays* the suspicions that everyone else has about the Limbo Man. It confuses the public at large who thinks it is able to identify people of a different sexual orientation because gay men don't get married? Right? Or even if they do, they don't stay married, right? Wrong.

Limbo Men stay married as long as their wives stay in limbo with them. Limbo Women are willing to fine tune their brains not to think about what they don't have. Rather, they try to focus on what they do have:

1. I have a nice home.
2. I have beautiful children.
3. I have friendly neighbors.
4. I have good in-laws who don't find too much fault with me (namely because you're covering up the family secret for them.)
5. I have a companion when I go on vacations.
6. I have a good friend.
7. I have a good friendship.
8. I have a husband who won't leave.

That's right, Limbo Woman, he won't leave. He's going to be by your side forever and ever because a Limbo Man doesn't leave. If he leaves, that means he might be dealing with whom he really is and what he does on the side might become front and center. This would upset the balance in his life and throw him out of the sphere of being emotionally straight. And that's a scary world that he just doesn't want to have to face. Life as a Limbo Man is too easy for him. It's also safe and secure.

Want to know something funny? Limbo Men think that their Limbo Wives know the truth—at least on some level. They think that all of the little clues that they have been confronted on prove that you know the truth somewhere in their Limbo Minds. And believe it or not, they feel that for this reason, you accept who they are. You can accept their little dalliances and dibs into that foreign world that neither of you really want to talk about. They think that your avoidance of the subject after a while is a form of acceptance. They don't see you running anywhere, and they also see you accepting that marriage can be built on friendship. You've given them the biggest gift of all—the end of sexual pressure.

You've learned how to live with them in Sexual Limbo—or abstinence. Your Limbo Libido has gone off into the distance—either with someone else or out the door or body. Whatever. He breathes a big sigh of relief. You are now the perfect wife.

Of course, you're not really the perfect wife. He still finds fault with you because you are a woman. And he is a gay man in disguise. It's never quite the right chemistry. He's never really happy living in between two worlds. He's comfortable, but never really happy. And he'll find ways to blame you for his unhappiness. It will be little things that make you feel stupid. After all, he thinks you're stupid. He thinks you know he's gay and you're willing to live with it. How smart could you be?

And so the years will pass. Your best years will pass in front of your eyes. Yes, the best years—those years where you could have been living a life without deceit, contempt, and sexual rejection. And before you know it, you'll look around and realize that you can't get back what you have lost. You'll never know how far you could have gone in life because you never had a cheering team cheering you on. You will never be inspired to write poems that have love and hope, but rather your poetry talks of sadness and loneliness. I suppose there is a market out there for poetry of the forlorn. Someone may be smart enough to publish a book on "Poetry for the Limbo Woman." It's sure to sell a million.

And so, my dear Limbo Women, my heart does go out to you. I feel as if you are walking in the valley of No Zone. Not quite here, not quite there. But the good news is that you can move into another time zone. You can join the freedom trail and look at life as a new adventure, just waiting for you. You can make a decision that you've had enough of Limbo Land and want to spend whatever remaining years you have finding yourself and a new sense of enjoyment. You can learn that life can be like a romantic comedy. You can laugh and love again no matter how old you are. Romance is never an age—it's a state of mind. And even though living with your Limbo man has dulled yours, you can still take your life back and live it the way you want to. You may not win the battle, but you can definitely win the war.

CHAPTER 7

AND SUFFER THE CHILDREN...

No one is more vulnerable than the innocent children that are born into straight/gay marriages. All children who come from unstable homes suffer, but often these children suffer more because they have additional problems to contend with than others.

There are several issues that are different with children from straight/gay marriages than in traditional marriages. The most important worry that straight wives have is wondering if there is an increased chance of their children being gay because of the gay father. This seems to be a reality from the statistics that I have compiled and studied over the years. As I mentioned earlier in Chapter 2, there is a higher occurrence of gay children born into straight/gay marriages. If you accept that homosexuality results from genetics, then this makes sense. It is estimated that 10% of the general population is homosexual. From less confirmed studies that have taken place, this statistic moves up to as high as 18% when a child has one gay parent.

I have heard debates through the years that this is due to role modeling by the gay parent, but I don't believe that to be true. If this was the case, why aren't all of the children in the family gay? Also, there are numerous gay fathers who never reveal their homosexuality and appear to be the most macho guys in the world. Whatever the reason, this is a real situation that families have to deal with.

The results can become very disheartening if the straight wife does not get past her homophobic feelings. If she is always downgrading gays, her gay child will find him/herself in the same situation as the gay father, trying to escape his/her homosexuality and spending years going through self-hatred and denial.

Another problem that children of gay parents face is the constant questioning of their sexuality throughout adolescence. The teenage years are the most difficult ones to deal with sexuality. Knowing that a parent is gay weighs heavily on the minds of teenagers who wonder whether this has been passed down to him/her. Even when the teenager is not gay, he or she fears that progression in age will lead to being gay. I have interviewed and counseled twenty-seven daughters of gay men who knew their fathers were gay prior to adolescence. The overwhelming majority suffered with this knowledge creating a situation where they became promiscuous to prove to themselves that they were straight. Their sexual activities started at a young age, as if they believed that having sex with men would make them straight.

Six of the twenty-seven daughters were lesbians and came to terms with it late in their teenage years or in early adulthood. These six women knew that they were different at a young age, but they were hoping that homosexuality was not what made them different. This is why they started having sexual relations with boys when they were between the ages of 13 and 15. Over time they were able to successfully accept their sexuality. Ironically, two of these women's gay fathers could not accept them being lesbians.

Most of the other females I spoke to claimed that they started having sexual relations long before they were ready just to make sure that they were "normal." This created more anguish because if they didn't enjoy the sex, they started to question if they were gay. They were too young to understand that teenage sex is often not fulfilling due to the inexperience of their male sex partners and the fact that their bodies and hormones are not fully developed.

Over time, I was able to find fifteen sons of gay men who were willing to discuss their emotions and feelings with me about their adolescent years. Eleven of the fifteen claimed to be straight, and one identified himself as bisexual. It seems as if the males had a much more difficult time dealing with their sexuality than the females. This was because of the way that society is socialized. Society is less accepting of a gay male than a lesbian female. It is also not unusual for adolescent boys to take part in some form of homosexual experimentation at least once, whether it be masturbating with a group of friends or fondling genitals of youthful playmates.

While other males just chalk it up to experimentation and rarely think about it again, sons of gay men think about it often, worrying that they are like their fathers. All of the sons told me that they became sexually active with girls at a young age to try to reassure themselves that they were straight, similarly the way that daughters of gay fathers reacted.

It was interesting to also note that the females were able to deal with their fathers' gay relationships much more easily than the sons were. Even if the daughters were not happy about seeing their fathers embracing a male lover, it didn't seem to put that much of a strain on the father-daughter relationships. The males, on the other hand, felt uncomfortable and even intimidated by their fathers' relationships once they reached adolescence, even if they knew the father's significant other prior to their teenage years. It is important to note that once most of the sons became adults, they were able to deal with their fathers' lifestyles better. By this time, they were secure in their own sexuality so it was easier to be accepting of their fathers and their fathers' lovers.

The children of the gay fathers had different feelings based on how their fathers handled their homosexuality and how they interacted with the children in general. Also, they were influenced by their mothers' reactions to their fathers' homosexuality.

Each person had a different level of acceptance. Some children could deal with the situation on an intellectual level, but when a father became involved in an actual relationship, the child was not able to deal with it. In straight relationships, the children may reject the new woman or man friend that a parent becomes involved with, but this is usually due to personality differences or jealousy on the part of the child. With a gay father, the rejection goes far beyond that point. It is not comfortable to see a father holding and caressing another man. It hits a negative cord in the brain as if it is something unnatural. Plus, with all of the homophobia in the world, we are taught from an early age that this imaging is deviant.

Children with gay fathers are usually ultra-secretive about their fathers' sexual identities. Some of the children of gay fathers that I've known have told me horror stories about other kids' reactions to them. This included acts of violence perpetrated by other teens, isolation from homes of friends, and refusal to be allowed to date peers by parents of the peers.

When I met the first members of my support group, Cindy and Ray, I also met their three children, Lori, 21; Marla, 19; and David,

16. Cindy's daughters were very outgoing like their parents and outspoken about the cruelty they suffered when people learned their father was gay.

Ray used to pick up men by hanging out in men's bathrooms in local department stores. He was very direct in his approach with anyone whom he thought might be interested in having a sexual encounter. Over the years, classmates of Lori and Marla frequently saw Ray pursuing men and concluded that their father was "a faggot," as he was called by the teenage boys who kept running into him in the department stores.

Both girls were beaten up repeatedly by high school peers who deemed them deviant because of their father. Their names were scrawled in the boys' bathrooms as being pigs and whores. In truth, both girls were very promiscuous because they wanted to make sure that they were straight and not gay. They needed to prove to themselves that they were not like their father. Their younger brother had an easier time because he was adopted and didn't worry about the genetic pool. He also entered high school after his sisters had graduated; people didn't realize who his sisters and father were.

Other children of gay fathers had similar experiences. They were ostracized, belittled, called names, isolated from their peers, labeled as gay when they weren't, etc. It's hard to believe that people are so ignorant, but it is true.

I will share an incident that happened when my children were young that forced me to stop doing television appearances. At that time, my son was in nursery school and my daughter was in kindergarten in a private school. I had done several national talk shows and various local shows about straight/gay marriages. I knew from the other members of my group that I was on a limited time line. Once my children were in regular public school the following year, I would not be able to appear on these shows anymore because they would suffer from the public backlash.

When the *Sally Jessie Raphael Show* producers asked me to appear on her show in 1986, I was leery because of my children. I explained my apprehension to the producer, but she reminded me that in Philadelphia at that time, the show was on at 5:00 a.m., even though it was shown on primetime morning hours throughout the rest of the country. She convinced me that thousands of people could be helped and minimized any possibility of damage to my children because of the remote hour of the local morning broadcast. I suppose I justified this in my own mind because I wanted to get the message to as many people as possible. Every time I did a television show, hundreds of letters poured in from women who were grateful for my message because they were living in an isolated hell with no one who understood their situation.

I went to St. Louis where the show was filmed. People always ask me if these shows pay you to be a guest. To my knowledge, they don't; however, they pay your travel, hotel, and food expenses. It gives people the chance to promote whatever causes they may be championing. Of course, over the years, some of the legitimate talk shows have turned into circuses for everyone and his brother who are seeking their fifteen minutes of fame. But in the 1980s, shows like *Donahue, Oprah,* and *Sally* were informational and informative and helped millions of people with different problems ranging from rare medical conditions to social ills.

Sally Jessie Raphael was a lovely person. She spent a few moments with me before the show to try to put me at ease. There was just one other guest on her show, and I had ample opportunity throughout the hour to talk about straight/gay marriages. As anticipated, I received hundreds of letters from all over the country from women in similar situations who finally understood what was going on in their marriages.

When the show was broadcast in Philadelphia, no one I knew mentioned to me that they had seen it, so I felt confident that there would be no repercussions. Several months later, my son, Alex, needed surgery because he had an infected lymph node. He was out of nursery school for two weeks. Before he returned, I received a call from the director of the school. She compassionately informed me that the parents of the children in Alex's class had petitioned for him not to be allowed to return. They based this on the conclusion that Alex had AIDS. One of the mothers had seen me on the *Sally* show, so she knew that Alex had a gay father. Then she found out that he was in the hospital for surgery and put the two pieces of information together concluding that if Alex had a gay father and was in the hospital, he must have AIDS.

In 1986, there was still a lot of unknown and misinformation about AIDS. People thought that you could contract AIDS just from breathing in the same air that an infected person was breathing. This one mother flamed the fires of the other mothers telling them that their children were at risk by playing with or sitting next to Alex in the same classroom.

Needless to say, I was horrified. The school administrator told the parents that they could take their children out of school, but she would not have Alex removed. I volunteered to remove Alex rather than have the school suffer, but the teachers were adamant that they would not be blackmailed by a modern-day witch-hunt. This was my awakening call. That was the last public program I appeared on, even though I had numerous offers from other top rated shows to be a guest. I knew if my children would be stigmatized at such a young age, they would go through school without friends and become the victims of ignorant parents and classmates.

I was always sympathetic with women whose husbands were openly gay in front of the children. They were not comfortable with their children watching their ex-husbands with other male lovers embracing and kissing. I understood that discomfort because I would have felt the same. Michael was involved with different men over the years, but he never demonstrated his affection for his partners in front of the children. He did not take them to gay events, gay meetings, gay father picnics, etc. Some fathers were insistent that their children attend these functions, creating a problem between the mothers and the gay fathers. If Michael *had* been that way, it would have put a tremendous strain on my relationship with him and the children's relationships with him.

I tried to be fair in my judgments of these matters. I understood the gay father's need to validate his new lifestyle. He had finally come to terms with his homosexuality and he was proud of what he was. He believed that his children should also be just as accepting of his lifestyle. He was tired of hiding and pretending and now that he was ready to be honest, he wanted to share that information with his children. He wanted his children to love him for who he was, even if it was different than what the children expected.

Of course, I understood the rage of the straight mother who not only had to contend with the news that her husband was gay, but was now left as a single parent with broken dreams and a broken marriage. Over time, many of these women could accept that their husbands were gay, but they did not want their children being dragged into the gay world. They couldn't understand why their ex-husbands who only had a few hours a week with the children couldn't spend quality time with them outside the gay community. They also felt that the gay lifestyle was being imposed on their children whether the children liked it or not.

Some mothers were fearful that other gay men would molest their children, and although I tried to reassure them that this was not the case, it often became a difficult argument. These stories were always fueled by groups like NAMBLA (National Association for Man-Boy Love) that promoted sex with children. Even though I showed evidence that there were straight groups with the same ideology, it didn't make much of an argument when there was so much publicity going on at the time about gay men wanting to molest boys.

I have met numerous gay men who are totally opposed to groups like NAMBLA. The thought of man-boy love is equally appalling to these gay men as it is to society in general. However, there is a lack of loud opposition on their part and I conclude this is because there are differences in the gay community's way of viewing the age of consenting sexuality. I did not find it uncommon for gay men to accept the concept of men having sex with teenage boys. Many of them projected back to their own teenage years when they wanted sex and felt it was perfectly normal to engage in it with an older, more experienced man.

Almost every gay man I have spoken to over the years admits to having a sexual encounter with an older man while he was a teenager. They also didn't feel that there was anything wrong or abnormal about it. Although this certainly happens with straight people, it does not happen nearly as often or is it classified as acceptable. In the straight world, people can accept teenagers having sex with other teens; but the thought of teenage girls or boys having sex with adults ten or more years older than them is not condoned. Even in a society where there is a double standard for females and males concerning sexual activity, it is still not socially acceptable for a teenage boy to be seduced by an older woman. Recently a female schoolteacher was jailed for having sex with a thirteen year old teenage boy while having his baby. Society has its limits, and once those limits are surpassed, there is little sympathy or understanding.

The issue of a gay parent is difficult enough for the gay parent and straight spouse to deal with. How much more difficult it must be for the child to deal with. The most important consideration for both parents is to think of the needs of the child first. For instance, if a child is uncomfortable with a father's homosexuality, the father should avoid thrusting the child into the gay arena. I knew gay fathers who insisted that their children participate in gay rights marches and rallies and carry signs with slogans such as "We Love Our Gay Fathers." Now this may look great for the cameras, but it makes the child very uncomfortable, fearing that peers in school may see the picture. Some children have no problem with their fathers being gay, but rather the insistence that the gay father has to announce it wherever he goes or when he is openly participating in the gay community. Once again, this leads to the issue of how the gay father handles his sexuality in front of the children.

I have seen bitter court battles with mothers fighting for sole custody and supervised visitation with the gay father because they are unable to deal with their ex-husbands' lifestyles. The fathers, on the other hand, are not willing to compromise when it comes to the needs of the children. They believe they can no longer live a lie and once they are involved in a relationship, they do not want to hide it from their children.

One gay couple, Don and Jack, tried to abide by the wishes of Don's ex-wife, Phyllis. Don was a strapping man of 6 feet four inches, who weighed 280 pounds. He had left Phyllis two years earlier after becoming involved with Jack, a slight black man who was half his size in weight, and at least one foot shorter in height. Don and Phyllis were both in their mid-thirties when their marriage ended. Phyllis was shocked when Don revealed that he was gay because he was the typical "macho" jock that she always worried would cheat with women.

Don had a strong personality and he was always flirting with the women. He later revealed that he was a flirt, but he was acting just to throw off anyone's suspicion. Don first knew that he was gay when he was in his teens. He had numerous sexual encounters with males. But the family pressure for a wife, children, business, home in the suburbs, etc. was intense, so he gave up the thoughts of leading a gay life. He met Phyllis when they were in their third year of college. Phyllis also had a strong personality, unlike the majority of other wives of gay men that I have met through the years. The two became fast friends because they shared numerous interests from politics to theater. After graduation from college, they married.

The first few years of the marriage were great. They loved each other's company, and even though their sex life was less than perfect, neither one of them cared that much about it. Phyllis had limited lovers before marriage, and she believed that marriage was the foundation for family and security. Sex was not a criterion to base a marriage on. Don performed sex with Phyllis as often as he thought he had to, which was usually once a month. He appreciated that fact that Phyllis was not one of those "nagging nymphos" as he called it. She was a "good wife" to him in that respect. What he didn't realize was that Phyllis thought he was unsatisfying in bed, which is why she didn't nag him. Her philosophy was that life was about a lot more than sex. It was about family and possessions, both of which Don could provide for her.

Don's family owned a successful furniture business that he inherited upon his college graduation. Phyllis became the mother of two children, Arlene and Russ, who were born two years apart, starting two years after the marriage. Don was a doting father and Phyllis was a controlling, but devoted, mother. They developed friendships with numerous couples who had children, and it was a weekly ritual to spend the weekends with at least two or three of these couples.

Don and Phyllis moved to a beautiful home on the Main Line on their five-year anniversary, and a number of their couple friends moved into the same development. To an outsider, this was the perfect family unit. A loving couple, two smart, adorable children, a house in the suburbs, great friends, a thriving business. Life was almost perfect—or at least Phyllis and the children thought it was.

Actually, Don was happy too. He and Phyllis were the best of friends. She never questioned him when he went out with the "guys." Of course, she was never suspicious that he was out having sex with the "guys."

Phyllis met Jack, the lust of Don's life, several years before the split-up. Don told her that Jack was the new assistant manager for the furniture store and the hardest worker that the store ever had. Jack was quiet but very likeable. Or maybe he just seemed quiet because Don was so overbearing. He was a frequent visitor in their household, and in time, Phyllis and the kids treated him like a member of the family.

Don and Phyllis could have led their lives like this for years, but Jack couldn't. He was tired of feeling like the third member of a crowd. Don had promised that in time, when the kids were older, he would tell Phyllis the truth and leave his happy home for a happier life with Jack. At the time, Jack thought he could deal with the arrangement, but after two years, he no longer could. He gave Don the ultimatum—"choose me or Phyllis, but you can't have both." With no choice but to choose, Don picked Jack.

Telling Phyllis the truth was the hardest thing that Don ever had to do in his life. He knew that his wife would not take this news well, and he also knew that there would be severe repercussions. But Don also knew that he had to be true to himself. He was very much in love with Jack and couldn't imagine life without him.

For weeks, Don practiced different ways to reveal this secret to his wife. Nothing sounded right because there was no way to soften the blow of the message. Don couldn't find the courage to have this kind of confrontation with Phyllis. In the end, he left her a letter explaining why he was leaving and just left.

Phyllis not only felt like a woman scorned but also like a woman burned. After twelve years of marriage, Don chose to leave her for a black man—a man who had spent countless times in their home with Phyllis treating him like a family member. She thought their perfect lives had been nothing more than a lie—a cover for the world to see. She felt used and violated. She didn't like being the brunt of this joke.

Don gave Phyllis the house, the car, a large support payment, and anything else she wanted that money could buy to try to make up for what he couldn't give her emotionally. Phyllis went on a buying spree, spending thousands of dollars to help her feel better about her life. Somehow, the usual high she always felt from spending didn't seem quite as exhilarating anymore.

During their first two months of separation, there was no verbal contact. Phyllis retained a lawyer within 24 hours and all communication was done by law firms. Don felt guilty for hurting his family, so he didn't pursue the issue of visitation rights in the beginning. Arlene was ten years old and Russ was eight at the time their father left. Phyllis didn't tell them the truth. She had no intention of informing her children that their father left her for a black man.

In spite of Don's guilt, he was happier than he had ever been during his marriage to Phyllis. Jack was his soul mate, his best friend, and his lover. Sex was exciting and fulfilling for the first time in his life. He never regretted making his decision to leave. Once they were on their own, Don and Jack decided to join a gay organization called Black and White Men Together. This was an organization where white men and black men who were attracted to each other could meet, socialize, politicize, and party. It didn't take long for Don and Jack to become leaders in the group.

Even though Jack was the love of Don's life, they both had sexual relationships with other men. Sometimes they did it together, sometimes separately. They both claimed that love had nothing to do with sexual activity. This seems to be an underlying philosophy in the gay community. I am not judging it, just acknowledging it.

After the first few months of separation passed, Don made a request to have the children stay with him and Jack one evening a week and every other weekend. Phyllis said the only way that she would allow this was if Don and Jack slept in separate bedrooms so that the kids would think they were roommates and not lovers.

This worked for Don and he felt it was the right thing to do for the children. For the first few months of visitation, there was no conflict.

One evening after a visitation, Arlene casually mentioned to her mother that when she woke up in the middle of the night and went into her father's bedroom, Uncle Jack was sleeping "naked" with him. Phyllis hit the roof. She felt sick to her stomach, imagining the worst scenario possible. When the children went to sleep, she phoned Don and called him every filthy name she could think of. Don apologized and promised it wouldn't happen again. Phyllis said she would never allow the children to sleep there again if it did happen. As the months wore on, Jack became annoyed that he had to sleep alone on the night that the kids were there. He felt as if they had become one big happy family unit and resented that fact that he had to pretend to be something he wasn't to appease Phyllis. This created tension between Don and Jack, and Jack threatened to end the relationship if Don didn't abide by his wishes. By that time, Don agreed that his sleeping arrangement was none of Phyllis's business. Jack was Don's true love of a lifetime and he wasn't about to sacrifice that for a nagging ex-wife. Anyway, his children loved Jack, and Don was convinced that they couldn't care less about who slept where. Although Don and Jack didn't flaunt their arrangements, they stopped hiding it.

Since Phyllis felt the need to cross-examine the children upon their arrival home on their weekends away, it didn't take long for her to find out about the new sleeping arrangements. At that point, she was determined to keep the children away from what she referred to as "insanity." She refused to allow any further overnight visits or even day visits. Don was infuriated and decided to take legal action.

Phyllis called in a panel of psychologists on behalf of the children, who all claimed that there could definitely be damage to the children's emotional state by being exposed to this kind of environment. Don was not expecting this attack and came unprepared. The court granted Don supervised visitation once every two weeks under the care of a social worker in a public place. In the 1980's, the political climate towards gay couples was less than positive, and courts often gave full rights to the straight mothers. Phyllis also had in her favor that Don and Jack were now the leaders of an organization called Black and White Men Together. The organization was a social/political group that focused on interracial gay relationships. Now it was not uncommon to have the house filled with male couples when the children were visiting, many of which were in compromising positions in front of the children.

These supervised visits continued for years until the children were old enough to determine if they wanted to spend more time with their father. By the time they were able to make the decision, it was too late. Their father died from AIDS.

When to the tell the children and who should tell the children are life-affecting issues and should be well thought out with all of the ramifications that can result from this news. Either parent might be anxious to tell the child for his or her own personal reasons, but it doesn't mean that the time is right for the child.

Is there ever a right time? Or rather, is there ever a good time? It depends on the maturity of your children and their ability to process this information. From my experience and the experiences of so many others in this situation, I would say that the period of adolescence is perhaps the least opportune time.

For instance, my daughter was more worldly and mature than my son, and I felt the need to tell her about her dad at an earlier age. Her father was not ready to tell her, and this created a terrible rift between us that lasted for almost a year. He felt it should have been his place to explain this to her when he was ready. I wanted him to tell her because by the time she was twelve years old, she was finding things in his house, including gay magazines and gay videos. Michael was also involved in a relationship, and my daughter would question why her dad was sleeping with another man.

He didn't want to tell her, but I didn't want her to think that the material she was finding in his home was the way of the world. I didn't want her getting distorted images of what sexuality was supposed to be like for her. Since Michael wouldn't tell her, I felt I had to tell her.

I am often asked what is the best way to approach children with this news. I think the way I approached it was with sensitivity and caring. There was no name calling—no aggressive accusations pointing a finger of blame. I sat my daughter, Stephanie, down and told her that we needed to have an important conversation.

I remember telling her that all people were born different, and that no two people are the same. Some people have blue eyes, some have brown. Some people have blonde hair, while others have brown and red. Some people have white skin, while others have brown skin. Most people are born straight and fall in love with people of the opposite sex. But some are born gay and fall in love with people of the same sex. I asked her if she knew any gay people. At that point, she had met some of my gay friends over the years and was able to name them. I never hid my gay friends' sexuality from my children because I didn't believe that I should have to lie about it if my friends were comfortable with their sexuality.

I asked Stephanie if she knew anybody who was gay besides my friends and she mentioned a couple of friends of Michael were gay. I explored her feelings about "gay" to see if she felt any negativity. I had tried my best over the years to raise my children in an environment of compassion and understanding for anyone who was different than they were because of my personal beliefs and convictions. As a result of this, my daughter was extremely liberal in her thinking about others and had no difficulty with someone because of his or her sexuality.

Having friends who are gay is much different than having a parent that is gay. The hard part was making the transition between people Stephanie knew who were gay and bridging that over to "your father is gay." After the words came out, they could never be taken back, and I knew that Stephanie's life would change forever after that information was revealed.

I emphasized the need to keep that information confidential because her peers would not be nearly as understanding as she was. Many people were ignorant when it came to homosexuality, and they would take it out on her if they found out. I had already learned the lessons of horrors from too many other children with gay fathers. I also asked Stephanie not to let her father know that I had told her about his sexuality because I knew he would be very angry. For six months, she kept this secret, but then she told her father that she knew.

At the age of twelve, Stephanie felt sorry for her father after finding out he was gay. It didn't bother her at that point as it would later on in her teens. She told her father because she wanted him to know that she loved him no matter what.

Needless to say, that was the one time in our relationship that Michael was the angriest at me. I never felt his anger and contempt the way I did on that day or over the next year while he refused to talk to me. And yet, I knew I had no choice but to tell our daughter.

Would I have told her under all circumstances? No. If Michael had not kept the evidence around or been involved in a relationship, I don't feel that there is a need to know. I have met some men through the years who never revealed their homosexuality to their children because they were leading visibly straight lives without suspicion. In that situation, why rock the boat? Of course, this is a decision that the gay parent needs to make depending on his comfort level with being gay.

I once met a man, Joe, who had left his wife when his children were teenagers because he could no longer live the straight lie. He told his wife, Rosa, the truth, and they both agreed for the sake of the children that it was better to keep that information private between themselves. Joe promised Rosa that he would never do anything to embarrass her or the children. If he had a relationship, the children would never meet the person, and there would never be any way for their three children to tell. It sounded like a feasible game plan.

Ironically, Joe and Rosa's oldest son, Vincent, was gay. He struggled with his homosexuality throughout his teenage years, fearing that if his family found out, he would be shunned. The family was active in their church where there was not much acceptance for homosexuality. Vince had always heard the not-so-subtle messages that gay was a sin. This added even more to his confusion about himself.

Vince had a solid relationship with Joe. As the first and oldest son, there had been a strong bond developed since birth. Joe knew his son was struggling with something, but was unable to get the information out of him. Joe told Vince that he could tell him anything—nothing could change his love for his son. But Vince was too hung up on fears of rejection to ever discuss it.

One morning, Rosa waited for Vince to come down to breakfast before school. When he didn't, she went into his room, assuming he had overslept. She found her son unconscious with a note. The note read, "Dear Mom and Dad, I could no longer live with the truth that I am gay knowing how it would destroy both of you. It is just easier to destroy myself. I love you, Vince."

Rosa started screaming and shaking Vince, but he did not wake up. She called 911 and then Joe, and they all were in the hospital within twelve minutes. Vince had taken a bottle of over-the-counter sleeping pills the night before but miraculously survived. Joe broke down hysterically crying and blaming himself for his son's homosexuality. Rosa also blamed Joe because she was so distraught at the moment.

When Vince regained consciousness, Rosa and Joe embraced him and explained that they loved him more than ever, and that Joe had something to reveal to him. Joe then told him the truth about his own sexuality. Although Vince felt relieved to know that his parents still loved him, he felt little comfort in the news that his father was gay. Vince also blamed his father for his homosexuality, and he couldn't understand why a gay man would want to produce children.

The family went for family counseling over the next eight months, and all of them learned to be open and honest in dealing with their feelings. In time, Vince understood why his father didn't reveal his secret—he was as fearful of rejection as his son was. Vince joined a support group for gay teenagers and in time was able to accept himself.

It is not unusual for teenagers to resent the fact that their fathers are gay, even if they grew up knowing the truth or were told prior to adolescence. Almost every teenager resents having a gay father on some level depending on the responsibility or lack of it on the part of the father.

One young lady, Gina, told me that her father repulsed her because he would hit on the guys she was bringing home. He would deny any such action, but she lost at least five young men in her life this way. After that, she secretly dated until she moved out of her house at the age of 18. I have heard similar stories from other daughters of gay fathers who are terrified about introducing their fathers to their boyfriends. They also share the fear of revealing their fathers' sexuality to boyfriends.

As I mentioned earlier in the chapter, there are often repercussions from parents who find out that their child is going with someone who has a gay father. Several of the daughters of gay fathers that I counseled told of relationships being destroyed by the pressures of the parents of their boyfriends once they learned that the girls' fathers were gay.

There are no easy answers to any of these issues. The most important advice is to learn to communicate. If your husband is gay, it is vitally important to have a heart-to-heart conversation about how and when to reveal this information to the children. The worst thing is for parents to use this information as a weapon against each other. I have heard wives threaten, "If he doesn't do this or that, I'm telling the kids that they have a faggot for a father." Who is the winner here? No one.

Children will have a difficult enough time dealing with this information, even if it comes out in a loving, accepting way. Teenagers are very homophobic by nature, and no one wants to be mocked or ostracized while they are growing up. This news changes lives because it creates secrets in the child, or sometimes even lies. It also creates an element of fear that the news will be revealed.

Parents must always keep in mind the need for safety and security of the children over their own needs of anger and revenge. As difficult as this may be, a straight mother should not discuss her own homophobic feelings with the children. For better or worse, this is the father of your child. What parents don't understand in general, not just relating to being married to someone gay, is that children always believe that they are made up of two parts—their mother and father. If they know that something is a problem with either parent, they believe that there is something wrong within them and this lowers their sense of self-esteem.

If a mother ridicules and criticizes the father because of his homosexuality, this will leave doubts within the children. They will start believing that there is something wrong within them, often causing behavior that is destructive.

As difficult as it may be, and believe me, I've had my moments of biting my tongue until it is double in size, try to keep your anger away from the kids. Call a friend, a relative, a hot line, a counselor, or anyone just to vent, but don't vent to the children.

Unlike my advice to men to reveal the information to your wife as soon as possible, when it comes to the children, there are some times that are better than others. It takes a lot of thought and consideration, but remember, the happiness and security of your children should always come first.

CHAPTER 8

BREAKING UP IS HARD TO DO

In the twenty-four years that I have counseled straight wives, the majority of them wanted to know why it is so hard to move on in their lives. Many of these women were paralyzed and afraid to make a move to end their miserable existence. Others were no longer in the marriages, but stuck in a maze of confusion, unable to move past the victimization phase and forward to a happier life. Let's discuss the causes of this problem and some solutions to show how to move forward.

Keep in mind I did not end my marriage. My ex-husband walked out in anger hoping that this would force me into further submission allowing him to do as he pleased. If Michael did not leave, I doubt that I would have done anything to hasten the breakup. I was part of a syndrome that so many women fall into when they are emotionally or physically abused. Although my ex-husband never lifted a hand to me or physically threatened me, I was mentally beaten beyond recognition. I used to criticize women who stayed in abusive marriages prior to that time, but I have since learned not to judge anyone's inability to walk away.

When I married Michael, I was a strong and independent woman. Within four years, I was a stranger to myself, my family, and friends who couldn't figure out what had happened to me. This is typical of so many of the women I have worked with. Living with someone who is consciously or unconsciously ripping away each layer of your self-esteem on a daily basis takes its toll on your sense of confidence and ability to think.

When women suspect or learn that their husbands are gay or "bisexual," they usually start blaming themselves because they don't understand homosexuality. "If only I was a better wife... if only I was better in bed... if only I was less demanding... if only I was more attractive, if only I was a better housekeeper, if only I was smarter, if only, if only, if only..."

All of these "if only's" only add to our list of why we feel that we are failures in the marriage. Most of us don't understand that this is not about us—it's about them. It's about our husbands' refusals to be honest with us and even with themselves. It's about placing the blame of the failed marriage where it correctly belongs—not transferring the blame to the unsuspecting wife to avoid honesty and responsibility. It is easier to fault the wife for the problems in the marriage rather than accept homosexuality as the cause of the problems.

Ending a marriage, even a bad marriage, is difficult at best. When you lack the self-confidence that usually results from these relationships, you are scared to make a move in any positive direction. I always advise women not to give up hope even when they believe it is impossible to escape. Map out a plan in your mind—short term. Don't worry about where you want to be years from now; organize a six-month or one-year plan. Be realistic. Accept that your bad marriage needs to end and map out the steps to do it at a pace that is convenient for you. If you believe that you are stuck with no choice, you lose all hope and just give up. Stop worrying about ways to keep a destructive marriage together and instead start thinking of the steps you need to take to live without your husband. Stop trying to force something to work that is not workable.

Millions of marriages with straight couples end in divorce, and women are able to begin relationships again without the added complications of straight/gay marriages. Why is it so much harder for us to move forward? There are several reasons.

1. THE SELF-ESTEEM ISSUE
Consciously or subconsciously, most wives blame themselves for their husbands' homosexuality, especially in the early stages of disclosure. It takes a full understanding of homosexuality to realize that in no way whatsoever are they responsible. When women learn that their husbands are gay, on some level they believe it was their failure that they were unable to "turn their husbands straight" or fulfill the needs of their husbands so those gay impulses would disappear. They continue to think the fault is theirs. After all, their husbands married them in good faith publicly

committing to a lifetime of marriage, family, and all the trappings that go along with the American dream. Their husbands made the choice to be in a marriage, have sexual relations, and proclaim their love. They "chose" to lead the straight life but somewhere along the way changed their minds. If men can have a "normal" life, why would they decide to act on their homosexual impulses? They acted happy when they got married, so why couldn't they remain happy?

When a woman believes that she is responsible for her husband turning to the opposite sex for physical and emotional pleasure, how much of a woman can she be? As long as a woman feels that she was the cause of her husband's sexual reversal, she will think that she can cause this to happen again in future relationships.

SOLUTION:

First, accept the fact that your husband was gay long before you came into the picture. He has no choice in his sexuality, and you had no influence as to when he would be able to accept and deal with it—if ever. Stop cluttering your mind with the "if only" syndrome. There is only one "if only" that could make a difference—"If only you were born with a penis." Other than this, there is nothing humanly possible that you can do to change the situation.

Next, try to remember who you were before the marriage. Dig deep into your memory and start making a list of all of your positive qualities and abilities, hopes, dreams, and aspirations that were and had before this relationship. Keep looking at them each day to remember who you really are, not what you have become because of this marriage.

Start rebuilding your self-esteem by doing things for yourself. Most women become so trapped during these marriages that they are afraid to do anything that will upset the delicate balance of existing day-to-day rather than living life and finding happiness. Look for something that will enhance your self-improvement such as returning to school, getting a job, showcasing your creative abilities, writing in a journal expressing your real feelings, or making new friends. Many women cut themselves off from a social and family life fearing they will be criticized or blamed by others. This is the right time to return to the support system you had before the marriage.

I suggest that women look for support groups that deal with women's issues if they are having difficulty moving forward on their own. If there is a support group for straight/gay marriages in your community, check it out. Make sure it is not one of those groups which urges you to stay in your marriage and accept it. In the next chapter, I will explain how to find or start these groups. If there are no organizations in your area for straight/gay marriages, join a women's group that focuses on self-esteem building, assertiveness training, and positive reinforcement. Some women need to see a professional therapist to help unravel the hurt inside that doesn't seem to go away. Don't be afraid to get this help. It can make a difference in your mental health and happiness, as well as your children's, in the years ahead.

2. THE LACK OF TRUST ISSUE

There are two issues here. The first is the lack of trust in your own judgment. After all, you were the one who married your husband thinking that he was straight. How could you have been so wrong? Why didn't you pick up the signs? How do you know that you won't make this mistake again? If you didn't know the first time, how can you be sure you'll know the next time around?

SOLUTION:

The chances are, it won't happen again. After reading this book, you have enough information to know what to look for as signs of a gay male. Keep reflecting on your own marriage and the signals that something was wrong. Check any stories that have inconsistencies when anticipating a new relationship. Don't ignore them for the sake of love. This is a good practice not only in for people coming out of a straight/gay marriage, but any kind of destructive marriage. Don't find yourself in a desperate situation where you are willing to settle for anyone who knows how to say, "I love you," just because you need to hear it. Avoid rushing into a relationship because of social or financial pressures.

After Michael left, I had no financial resources and went on welfare for three years. I had two young children and I was emotionally out of synch. I took that time to repair myself mentally, go to college, earn my degrees, and move on to a happier life. I struggled financially for a long time, but I had peace of mind because each night when I went to bed, I knew that I could wake up the next day and think about a future. Throughout my marriage, I often went to bed crying because I was miserable and woke up the same way. I existed day to day—I wasn't living.

It took me many years to trust myself enough to think about a relationship again. Each of us moves at a different pace. Some women make the drastic mistake of jumping into a relationship much too fast. They don't end up with a gay husband, but they could end up with the wrong husband or relationship. Give yourself time to reconnect with who you are first. Learn that you can function independently as a person. Start rebuilding those torn away layers of self-esteem you had before the marriage, or in some cases, start building the self-esteem you lacked before the marriage.

Don't listen to the well-meaning advice of those around you who keep pressuring you to find a man again. There are people who still believe you can't be happy in life until you are a couple with someone. They will try to set you up with their friends, family members, co-workers, etc. because they believe this is the only way you can be happy. Don't be afraid to say that you are not ready to meet someone because you need time to work on yourself and resolve the issues to make you complete again. Most of us in this situation are used to being "people pleasers," meaning that our need to make others happy comes before our need to make ourselves happy. This is a red-flag sign of low personal self-esteem.

The other trust issue is the one of being able to trust a man again. Throughout the marriage to your gay husband, you were lied to, cheated on, blamed for things that were not your fault, and led to believe that you were the cause of the problems in the marriage. Is this a general trend in all men? How do you know that the next man won't do the same things to you?

SOLUTION:

Certainly this is a more difficult problem to answer. Finding a good man is a universal problem—not exclusive to ex-wives of gay men. I have counseled straight couples over the years who had bad marriages and/or relationships. There are numerous variables that determine the success of any relationship. There are no guarantees through the years no matter how certain you are about someone being the right mate at any time in your life.

The one encouraging piece of information I can tell you is that I do know couples who have wonderful marriages. These are marriages where trust is developed at an early stage and continually worked on. Every couple has its shares of arguments and problems, but that is human nature. It doesn't mean that you don't love a person or can't trust a person when this happens. No two people are identical, and to think that you can find someone who will always agree with you about everything is unrealistic and not what a caring relationship is about—it's what a controlling relationship is about!

Look for someone who shares your value systems. Never take a relationship for granted by assuming it will remain intact. It needs nurturing at all times. Don't be afraid to say, "I love you," or to express what your needs and desires are—including sexually. Talk to couples who have solid marriages and see what makes them successful. I always like to ask these couples how they keep their relationship happy and their love growing. It gives me inspiration to see that relationships can work. It's wonderful to see how positive a relationship can stay when *both* partners think about the needs of each other—not just one partner wondering how to please the other one.

3. THE SEX ISSUE

The most difficult challenge for me personally was to have sex after the end of my marriage. Any kind of sexual confidence or enjoyment I had in the past seemed to fade from my memory. I felt like a sexual failure even when I knew that I was not responsible for my ex-husband's homosexuality. I was afraid to try again. I thought that I would be a disappointment to any man like I was to him. Some women jump right into the water just to start believing in themselves again sexually. Others block it from their minds like I did until the timing is right.

SOLUTION:

Trust me when I tell you that making love with someone you care about or love is the most wonderful experience in the world. I know because I have been blessed with this for the past fourteen years after waiting over a decade after my marriage to find it. You don't have to wait until you fall in love again—you can have great sex with someone whom you feel a physical attraction to and when the chemistry is right. This can help to reassure you that you are a "normal" woman—not a nymphomaniac or bad sex partner as your gay husband led you to believe.

Although sex is not the most important factor in a relationship, it is a very important one because it builds on the intimacy in a relationship. Without it, you may as well be living with a brother or cousin. Some women are willing to settle for that, but remember, you are settling. I say you deserve more.

For many of us, having sex for the first time after our marriages was a frightening step to take because of our fear of failure. It is no surprise that if a woman has an unfulfilling sexual experience with the next man in her life, she personalizes it as her fault. After coming out of a marriage where you were led to believe that unfulfilling sex was your fault, it is understandable. We forgot, or in some cases of sexual inexperience never knew, that not every straight man is a great lover or is interested in pleasing a woman. There are plenty of men who are only interested in pleasing themselves, and they assume that you are feeling just as good as they are at the end of the encounter or they just don't care. Practice communicating with your partner that you are not satisfied just because he is. Women by nature are not assertive, and expressing your sexual needs is one of the most difficult obstacles. It took me years of bad sexual experiences to be able to say, "This is what makes me happy." If you have a responsive lover, he will remembers this. If you have a lover who overlooks this or doesn't care—well, forget him and cut your losses. You've already paid your dues with unfulfilling sex in your marriage.

4. THE ISSUE OF ACCEPTING YOUR EX-HUSBAND'S GAY LIFESTYLE WHEN THERE ARE CHILDREN INVOLVED.

When a straight marriage ends, there can be complications resulting from the husband's new choice in companionship. The ex-wife wonders if the new woman will treat her children with kindness during the visitations and if they will accept a new woman in her husband's life. For ex-wives of gay men, the issues are far more complicated. Many women are petrified by the thought of the children being exposed to the homosexual lifestyle. Although most ex-wives eventually accept that homosexuality is not a choice that a man consciously makes because it is not a matter of choice, it doesn't mean that they are any more comfortable facing the situation. The emotions run very high here ranging from the fear that the children will somehow be influenced by the gay lifestyle to the fear that the male children will be physically molested by the gay friends or lover of the ex-husband.

There is always a fear of the unknown. To many women, the only thing they know about homosexuality is that it wrecked their marriage, and they don't want to give it a chance to destroy their children. Society promotes the message that homosexuality is perverted, distorted, and deviant. How can women come to terms with their children around this lifestyle?

SOLUTION:

I wish I had a clear-cut answer for this problem, but I don't. The best advice I can give you is to try to communicate with your ex-husband about what is best for the children. In many of my counseling experiences, the gay husband understands the need for the children not to have to his lifestyle displayed because it creates confusion. There are so many factors to consider here including the age of the children, the location of the family, the acceptance of homosexuality by the woman, and the financial and emotional support given by the gay father.

I was fortunate that my ex-husband was careful around our children not to expose them to situations that they were too young to understand. As they grew older, I was the one who revealed the information at a time that I felt it was necessary. Michael was very angered by this because he didn't want them to know, or at least to find out from me. Children today are far more educated and perceptive on these issues than we were growing up. I did not want them to be confused by mixed messages. As they grew older, they were like most kids and natural curiosity led them to rummage through gay books and films hidden in Michael's home. They started asking me questions, and although I avoided answering directly for as long as possible, there came a time when I knew they had to know the truth. I explained the situation with great sensitivity, thought, and compassion, but when Michael found out, it caused a rift that lasted nearly a year.

I don't regret making that choice because as I explained in an earlier chapter, sexuality during adolescence is confusing under any circumstances. I also knew from doing research that the chances of having a gay child with one gay parent were higher due to genetics. I never wanted my children to ever feel self-hating or confused about themselves if this turned out to be the case.

Many women fear that their children will be psychologically damaged when they find out about the father's homosexuality. If handled correctly by both parties, this doesn't have to happen. Gay fathers need to understand that it took them years to come to terms with their homosexuality, and now that they have, they can't expect the children or wife to deal with it at the moment they can accept it.

There are some wonderful gay role models in society, and I suggest that you start finding some of those whom your children can relate to whether it is writers, musicians, actors, scientists, sports figures, or politicians. Don't dwell on the sensationalism of homosexuality that creates the stereotype that society magnifies as being typical.

You can learn about the gay community without immersing yourself in it. Too much exposure in this case can cloud your judgment and jade your opinion. You can be accepting and understanding of a different lifestyle without judging it. The gay world is different than the straight world. Values are different in some respects, but in other cases, the same. Bottom line—gay people want the same things that straight people want—to find love, happiness, and a sense of self-worth in a society that will always suffer from homophobia.

The one thing I do know is that being around gay people will not change the sexual orientation of your children. If you fear that gay is "contagious," stop thinking it. Your children have no more chance of becoming gay from being in the company of gay people than they have of becoming a different color from socializing with people of a different color. The gay community does not proselytize or prey on straight boys to become gay. Individuals may fantasize or express their desires to be with a straight male, but in most cases that's where it ends. Pedophilia is far more prevalent in the straight community than it is in the gay community. The irresponsible actions of individuals cannot be held against the community any more than the actions of individuals of any group of people.

When men in the gay community proclaim they are "proud to be gay," this is a statement of self-worthiness rather than a conscious effort of conversion to a lifestyle. Like all oppressed minorities, gay people are looking for acceptance—first by themselves, then of others.

Keep in mind when it comes to children, the security of the child feeling loved by both parents is foremost in importance. Make every effort to keep the gay father involved in the lives of the children. Positive parenting should be the main issue—not the sexuality. When either party loses sight of this, the children are the real losers.

All of this is good advice, but sometimes you have a father who is not cooperative with communicating with you and doesn't care about your feelings or your children's feelings of discomfort. As I mentioned in an earlier chapter about the actions of a leader of the Gay Father's Coalition who insisted on taking his son to gay outings, marches, and picnics, do what you have to do to protect your child from feeling uncomfortable. You do have rights as the mother, and in most cases, the primary caretaker, to fight for the well-being of your child's mental health. If this means taking the issue to court, then do it.

CHAPTER 9

BISEXUALITY---ILLUSION AND DELUSION

I hear it all the time and I've heard it for years. "My husband is not *gay*, he is *bisexual.*" Or, I hear from the husbands that, "There's no way I am gay; I have bisexual tendencies." When I first started counseling wives and straight/gay couples, I would get angry when those words would start the conversation after the informal pleasantries. I was in the beginning stages of my own recovery, and my anger from the lies and deceit of my ex-husband during our marriage was still too fresh in my mind. But now, years later, I can calmly discuss this issue with objectivity and understanding because most of my pain and anger is gone. I do admit, though, that the whole issue still irritates me.

Let's talk reality. What is bisexuality anyway? A married gay man who has sex with his wife but still sexually desires a man? A man who lives a straight life with a wife and children to shield him in public while he has homosexual encounters on the side? A man who claims he is attracted to both men and women but still needs a man when he's with a woman? I think not. **Bisexuality is an excuse.** For gay men it is an **illusion,** creating a picture that allows them to fit into the straight world. For their straight wives it is a **delusion,** creating a justification for keeping the marriage together.

If straight/gay couples choose to keep their marriage together for whatever reasons, that is a choice they make. But the problem with using bisexuality as the justification only postpones the inevitable of facing the real issue. I say this at the beginning rather than the end because it is important to keep this thought in mind while you sift through the following discussion.

First, let's look at the overall picture. Most women don't understand homosexuality. I didn't. I thought a gay person is attracted to someone of the same sex. That's what I learned from an early age, and no one disputed those facts. Yes, I heard about movie stars that married and turned out to be gay. But those were

Hollywood stories, and in the movies, anything goes. It didn't have any sense of reality to me. I recognized gay people once I reached my mid-to-late teens. Everyone could identify them because they always stood out. The gay guys were effeminate and flamboyant. They always had girl friends around them, but no girlfriends. Girls loved them because they were wonderful confidants, advice givers, and fashion experts. They would gossip with you, help you fashion your hair, and confirm whether or not your choice in men would have been their choice.

And we never understood what made men gay, we only knew it was wrong. We couldn't visualize two men being passionate together like we were with the men we fell in love with. We could intellectualize it, but we couldn't imagine it without thinking there was something sick and demented about it. There was no way we could ever suspect that we could marry someone gay and not know it.

So how did it happen? How could something that seemed so clear become so jumbled and confusing? How could our judgment be so off-target? Easy. It was our misconception of "gay." We didn't know that there were gay men who had the ability to perform sexually with a woman even though it was certainly not a preference. Not all gay men can do this, but some can. Does it mean they want to have sex with a woman? Not really. Given the choice, they are not going to pick you. But the problem is, those gay men who can perform with women believe they don't have a choice.

These men are caught between two worlds and are really lost. They are emotionally straight, but physically gay. They don't emotionally fit into the gay world, and they are hoping that their ability to perform heterosexually will take away the nagging physical attraction they have for men. They can't come to terms with themselves because they too have been taught that there is something morally wrong with being gay. And so they live a lie, living it with you and resenting you for it. They misplace their own frustrations on their wives and express it through anger and hostility where it hurts the most.

Some husbands do come to terms with their homosexuality at some point, but there is no way to predict when this will happen.

A year, two, ten, twenty, forty—I've seen it take place at all different times. But many married gay men are never able to give up the comfort and safety of living in the straight world, even if it isn't quite as comfortable as they would like it to be. The challenge alone of finding ways to avoid sexual relations with your wife has to be exhausting. No matter how difficult living a lie may be, it is easier than being part of the gay world. How do they know that? Because they have explored the gay world, even if it is from a distance. They tested the waters, putting in one toe at a time, never able to submerge the whole foot.

The gay world wasn't something they could identify with—it was a bunch of freaks who blatantly bragged to the outside world that they were proud of this fluke. It lacked sincerity, commitment and depth. Everything was focused on one thing—sex. They saw public displays at the gay bars where men embraced each other and passionately kissed. They watched men dancing together and grinding their bodies in a lewd manner. They were approached by young male prostitutes on the streets in gay neighborhoods offering all kinds of sexual services for money. They read the gay newspapers and looked through the personal ads which may have sexually excited them but emotionally repulsed them. And what they saw, they hated. They were overcome with a sense of shame and revulsion. This was definitely not who they were. And so they ran back to the safety net. They ran home to their marriage, thinking of ways to fulfill those deepening urges without revealing their identity.

At some point, these men find the opportunity to act on their homosexual needs and they think it's okay. Why? Because they're not gay—merely "bisexual." Big deal. What does it have to do with you anyway? It's not like they're cheating on you with another woman. You should feel better about that. Don't take it personally. It's just a character flaw that you can learn to live with. If you really love your husband, you should be willing to overlook his little male indiscretions and his occasional weaknesses that he has no control over.

And then there is you, the wife who finally learns what is ripping apart your self-esteem day by day. Now it all makes sense. Your husband is *bisexual.* You were worried it was another woman. You may have even suspected that your husband was homosexual. What a relief! Here you thought divorce was looming overhead for reasons unknown but now you know that this is a workable problem. Bisexual. You have a fighting chance to make the marriage work. Right? Wrong!

When my ex-husband alluded to being "bisexual" during one (and only one) conversation in our marriage, I wasn't exactly stunned. There were hints building up over time that pointed me in that direction, so it was somewhat of a relief when he didn't blow up or dispute my accusation. Bisexual. It sure sounded and felt much better than "homosexual" which was my greatest fear. I could work with "bisexual" because it meant I had a chance of pulling my husband over the middle line to my side of the fence. All I had to do was make myself into the dream wife that would make him forget about looking elsewhere. I could take away those twinges of desire he felt for men by becoming more attractive and loving. And I justified that I could live with this problem as long as it was under my terms and conditions. In the spirit of compromise necessary in every good marriage, I made my list.

1. If you have to go out every six months or so to take care of your business, I can live with it.
2. As long as you satisfy whatever needs you have with someone of consenting age, I can live with it.
3. As long as I never have to know anything about this phase of your life, I can live with it.

I had it all wrapped up in a neat package. My husband gave my conditions a nod of acceptance, and we stated that we would never discuss it again.

Of course, this agreement was pushing me even further into the state of delusion. Once I knew that my husband wanted to have sex with men, it didn't matter what the classification of his sexuality was. I started obsessing and panicking every time he walked out the door without an explanation. Was this going to be the day? Who was he with? If he was bisexual, why couldn't I satisfy his needs? That's the problem. Intellectually we can filter the information that we are not at fault, but when your husband engages in sex with a man, emotionally we don't believe it. Although your husband justifies to himself that it's not cheating because it's a man, after a while you can't. Infidelity is infidelity. Cheating is cheating. Do you feel better that he's bestowing his passion on a man—the passion he's never had for you?

I was scared and nervous once I faced the truth. I didn't want to break up my marriage. I loved my husband even though he treated me with contempt. I could never do anything right in his eyes because subconsciously, I stood between him and his happiness. I was cramping his style, but as time went on, he grew bolder and stopped caring about what I thought. Throughout our marriage, my husband denied being gay. After our "bisexual agreement," he denied admitting to anything; he claimed he just went along with my paranoid thoughts to placate me. By this time it was harder to fool me. I knew the signs like the glances at attractive young men that lasted far too long or the camaraderie with males that far exceeded the boundaries of friendship.

After the breakup of my marriage, my husband was able to jump into the water full force and tried to find his place in the gay world. He wasn't sure where he belonged although he had been physically part of that world for years before I met him. He had a love/hate relationship with the gay community. He knew what he wanted sexually, but found the gay lifestyle empty. The straight lifestyle offered him a security blanket. A loving wife, adorable children, respectability, stability -- who wouldn't want that? For gay men who marry, they believe they can have the best of both worlds—the American dream plus an extra dream on the side. But at what expense to that devoted wife who trusts him to be honest and faithful?

Believe me, I am sympathetic to women who are scared to face the truth. I was one of them, and it was the most difficult struggle I've ever dealt with. My ground rules of what I could live with kept changing as my husband became bolder and less secretive. And each time I had to modify those ground rules to his advantage, I became more broken down mentally because I was giving in to something that I couldn't accept—a way of life that was unacceptable in a marriage. The worst part was that I believed it was *my* personal failure. If my husband was bisexual, I must be doing something wrong or otherwise he would want to be with me instead of a man.

Most gay men are wonderful to their wives when they feel an overpowering sense of guilt for their indiscretions. They are not looking to intentionally hurt their wives, and much like the abuse syndrome, all kinds of promises of change and reform are made when they are caught. It's like the honeymoon is starting all over again, giving the wife a false sense of desperately needed hope. The husband becomes loving, giving, and even semi-passionate for a time to prove that his little mistake is in the past and should be forgiven and forgotten. But it usually doesn't take long before the big pull starts. That's just the way it is when nature takes its course. And each time it happens, the wife becomes more alert to the warning signs and can almost anticipate what's around the corner when her husband leaves the house.

It all comes down to what you are willing to live with. If your husband is having sex with men, you can call it whatever name you want, but as the old saying goes, a rose by any other name is still a rose. A man who has sexual relations with a man is still a gay man in my book. And a final warning for those of you whose husbands keep reassuring you that they have these gay attractions but never acted on them. Don't believe it. In almost all cases, they have acted on their needs either prior to or during your marriage. They may claim that they are just watching gay porno movies or reading gay magazines to satisfy these urges, but that's usually a ploy to make you feel better and throw you off track.

I have met hundreds of gay husbands in marriages, leaving marriages, and after their marriages. At some point during their marriage, most of them were having gay sex in one form or another through casual dating, one-night stands, or full-fledged relationships and lying to their wives to "protect" their marriage. We desperately want to believe the lies they tell us. Even when the truth is smacking us right in the face, we believe their excuses because the truth is too painful to accept. We build a layer in our subconscious that I refer to as "limbo"—a state of mind where we exist day to day without living life because we are hurting too badly. And some women are able to live their lives this way indefinitely rather than give themselves the chance at real happiness and fulfillment. I understand this. Sometimes we are so mentally weakened from dealing with this horrific situation that we feel unable to stand up and make a change. Certainly I am not one to judge when a woman is ready, if ever, to make that move. I don't know if I would have had the courage and confidence to make that choice if my ex-husband didn't make it for me. When you lose all of your self-confidence and self-worth, it's hard to believe that you even deserve a chance at happiness. And so you walk through the days and nights sitting in limbo waiting for a miracle because you don't have the strength to realize that you can walk away from this trap.

The only way you will ever regain any of your mental strength back is to stop making excuses for your husband's gay behavior by labeling it "bisexual." Look at things for what they are and don't let him tell you otherwise. If he wants to keep fooling himself, fine, but don't let him keep fooling you. Each day that you can say, "my husband is gay," you will find yourself growing stronger because you can look at your marriage for what it is—not what it's not or not what you wish it could be. Only then will you be able to start thinking about the right move for yourself, your future, and your long-deserved happiness in the world of the living, not the world of existing.

Chapter 10

Happily Every Re-After

There's no point writing and now revising a book unless I can finish it with a happy ending. That's what my work is about—giving people hope for happy endings. I have asked five women from my online support group to write for this chapter because I intend to inspire those of you who want to believe that life can be better. I presented them with a series of questions, and here are their responses. First, a little information about my friends:

GRETCHEN

Gretchen, 48, is the mother of a son, 9, and a daughter, 8. She lives outside of Denver, Colorado. Gretchen is technical writer and trainer, currently working at a large hospital. She was married to her gay husband for eight years before they divorced and he was able to come to terms with his homosexuality. As her marriage was ending, Gretchen met another man who was also going through a divorce. Their friendship grew and culminated in their marriage in February, 2003.

BECKY

Becky, age 42, is a mother of a son 10 years old and a daughter who is 13. She was married for 9 years when she discovered that her ex husband had an affair with a man, whom he moved 1000 miles to live with. That was 7 years ago, and her divorce has been final for 4 years. I am a full time mom and work part time as a nurse.

LINDA

Linda, age 56, was stunned when her husband came out to her on their 29th wedding anniversary. By their next anniversary, they were divorced. They have two sons, who were 15 and 19 when the divorce occurred. Linda worked many years as a news reporter, but is now the gardener for a private plantation near Charleston, South Carolina.

GRACE

Grace, age 42, is mother to 4 children, 2 natural sons, ages 22 and 24. She also has 2 chosen children who are profoundly handicapped, with extensive medical needs, ages 19 and 7. She lives in Alberta, Canada. She was married for 25 years.

CONNIE

Connie is a 38 year old mother of three boys, ages 10, 9, and 8. She works as a Systems Administrator. She was married for 13 years, and left her marriage in 2003. Her divorce was finalized in 2004.

1. **How long were you married to your gay husband?**
    Gretchen - We were married for over eight years (our last wedding anniversary was Sept. 11, 2001 – how appropriate!), and dated for five years before that.
    Becky - At the time of our divorce we had been married 11 years and 10 months.
    Linda - 29 years.
    Grace - We are currently going thru the final divorce process. We have been married just shy of 25 years.
    Connie - 12 years, 10 months and 13 days.

2. **Did you have any clue that he was gay when you married him?**
    Gretchen - It's so funny, but the very first time I met him, while we were in graduate school, I thought was that he was gay. Nevertheless, he started to call me all the time, then pursue me to date him, so I dismissed that thought. How could a man be gay if he wanted to date a woman? If I had any suspicions, I definitely repressed them. I was getting older, maybe a little desperate to marry and have children, and he was my best shot. Of course, hindsight is 20-20 and in retrospect, so many things about him, his personality quirks, his effeminate behavior, scream out "GAY!" Certainly, many of our mutual friends held the same suspicions, as I found out later.
    Becky - No, no clues at all. Not even any retrospectively.
    Linda - Before we were married, he told me that he'd fooled around with one of his college roommates. He explained that he'd walked in on his roommate and found him masturbating. He and the roommate jerked off together. He went on to assure me that he really didn't think he was gay, that he and his roommate were just horny 18-year-olds jerking off at a sexually repressed Southern Baptist college. I accepted his explanation at face value. I was 20 years old. I was a college graduate, but I had no idea what "homosexual" or "gay" really meant.
    Grace - I knew when we were first married that he was *awkward* around other men, but I had no clue as to why. He

was complaining to me within the first three months of our marriage, that I was *boring* to him sexually.

Connie - Yes, my cousin told me that my husband was gay before I married him, but I didn't believe him.

3. **At what point in your marriage did you realize that he was gay?**

Gretchen - It wasn't until I got him to agree to divorce me that the light finally went on over my thick head. It was actually my current husband (we were casual friends at the time) who gently suggested that I think about that aspect of him and how that might explain why he was such an unhappy man without any real reason to be. The key indicator was that my gay husband's father was also gay; he came out right before he died of AIDS. I am a firm believer that homosexuality is an inborn trait, and is most likely genetically linked. I then began to research the subject on the Internet and immediately found Bonnie's website. I will never forget the flood of emotion I felt as I read page after page of evidence that all pointed to the same conclusion. I was relieved to finally have an answer as to why this man was acting the way he did; I was also initially very ashamed that I completely missed what his problem was and angry at myself for being so desperate that I had to marry a fag!

Becky - When I found some thoughts he had written down in his day timer comparing me to a man he had met in a bar, while out of town at a meeting.

Linda - I never suspected him until he came out to me on our 29th anniversary.

Grace - I didn't actually realize that he might be gay until we'd been married for 21 years, although it would have been buried deep in my mind. I went into counseling after suffering a nervous breakdown, and it just came out of me, that I thought he might be gay. As I talked through everything with a psychologist, I realized there had been many signs throughout the marriage. His avoidance of sexual intimacy, dressing up and perverted sexuality were at the top of the list. Pornography and work addictions were also right up there. The psychologist called these things "homosexual tendencies."

Connie - About two years into the marriage, I realized that I was the only one initiating sex and affection. I thought something was wrong with me. I started to feel rejected.

4. **Did you confront him with your suspicions? If yes, did he deny it?**

Gretchen - Just as Bonnie counsels, I decided to confront my ex-husband right away after reading her website. I wanted to be sure to do my best to elicit an honest reaction from him and not to scare him into silence. What I told him was that I thought he was *unsure* about his sexuality and that it was making his life very difficult. I made it clear that I didn't judge homosexuality negatively, that it's something you can't do anything about. He didn't react much to my statements and neither confirmed nor denied having homosexual feelings, which in my mind was an admission. He did adamantly declare that he had never acted upon his feelings with other men, which I have no reason to disbelieve. Our confrontation is the best thing that could have happened to him, I believe. He is finally able to address these long-suppressed feelings and finally discover who he really is.

Becky - About five days after reading what he had written down, I did confront him. He didn't deny it, since it is kind of difficult to deny your own words.

Linda - Not applicable.

Grace - Yes, he denied it, but he was very unsure. He now shares a house with a young man.

Connie - Yes, on August 7, 2002, he denied it.

5. **What gave you the strength to leave the marriage and ask for a divorce? How did he react?**

Gretchen - In retrospect, our marriage was never really very strong, and it just got worse as time went on. His lack of respect for me degenerated into verbal, then physical abuse. Even though I was very unhappy for many years, it took me quite a while to even consider divorce. I had two small children and a beautiful house in the suburbs; I was very reluctant to even think about giving it all up, even though I am a professional working woman with an MBA, with the means to support my children and myself. I think what I hated to give up most was the <u>fantasy</u> of having it all; a loving family and the material goods I never had growing up.

My ex-husband was actually very resistant to divorce, claiming that if only I changed, then everything would be all right. Of course he didn't want a divorce, even if it meant living with me, someone who he thought was unattractive, inattentive to domestic chores, etc.! He was living his fantasy as well – to be a straight man in a straight world!

Becky - Fortunately, I had a wonderful counselor we were seeing and she encouraged him to move out and actually encouraged me to file for divorce which actually took me about 10 months to do. She felt he shouldn't live in the house when he was behaving the way he was and not committed to our relationship. I actually didn't get mad enough or the courage to stand up for ME to file for divorce until he announced he was moving 1,000 miles away to be with his boyfriend! The therapist we were seeing was about the only person at the time that my gay husband would listen to and respect her opinion. He therefore moved out of the house and listened to what she said about the reasons for the separation, without much resistance.

Linda - I don't know exactly. The night he came out to me, the scales were lifted from my eyes and my hindsight was 20/20 and I knew in my heart that our marriage was finished. Suddenly I saw things that he had done and said over the past 10 to 15 years in a new light. I had an "Ah ha!" moment. At the same time, I felt as my body had been torn in two. I was in a state of shock.

The next day, I asked him to move out immediately. He had just opened an art gallery in the first floor of an old Victorian house. He moved into his office on the second floor and made it into an apartment.

Both he and I were in shock for the first three months of our separation. He swore that he stilled loved me, but that he was going nuts trying to repress his true nature. My response to him was that I loved him always, but that I was not interested in a non-monogamous marriage.

Seven months after our separation, I told John that I was filing for divorce. He thought we should take things more slowly, however, he said he did not want to give up the possibility of intimate relations with men. That being the case, I said there's no reason to delay this divorce. I even stretched the truth about the date he moved out so that I could file for the divorce three months early. (South Carolina has a one-year waiting period between separation and filing for divorce.) Our divorce was made final 13 months after he came out to me.

Grace - I told him I wanted a divorce when I had my breakdown. I just didn't realize why I wanted away from him at the time, just that I was desperate to be away from him. He was extremely angry! At the time, I was also involved in counseling with a psychologist provided for by Social Services. When the abuse issues against me came to there attention, I had to make a decision. Either he had to go or I would lose the children in my care. The decision was an easy one for me.

Connie - I read Bonnie's first book, *Is He Straight?* and I saw my whole life in that book. Then Bonnie sent me her second book. Everything I read pertained to my life and I knew if I ever wanted to be happy again, I had to leave. He was very angry, started blaming me for not being a good wife and mother. He accused me of having an affair. Then he moved into the guest room (that was my confirmation that he was truly gay). A real man would never react like that.

6. **Was your husband emotionally or physically abusive in any way while you were married?**
   Gretchen - YES. I can't believe the years of verbal and sometimes physical abuse I put up with. I have always been 40-50 pounds overweight, and had been subjected to years of nagging and cajoling to lose weight, even after two therapists told my husband how counterproductive that behavior was. My husband was hypercritical about many other aspects of our

life together as well, to the point where friends and relatives would comment on his disrespect towards me. The physical abuse was occasional and not severe, but two incidents in two months truly got me going to end the marriage.

I now recognize a pattern in his abuse. He would go through mood cycles, slowly building up to a confrontation that required many hours of argument about insignificant things, often going back years. Then, once he got it out of his system, he would be a totally loving, affectionate husband until his mood started to give way again. It was an awful way to live, walking on eggshells around him. I realize now that his repression and denial had such a tremendous psychological affect on him. I was the perfect foil; by having someone to criticize and focus on, he could avoid focusing on himself. Since he has now reached a certain degree of acceptance of his sexuality, the confrontation cycles have stopped!

Becky - I would have to say emotionally abusive towards the last three to five years of the marriage. I never did it right or well enough and EVERYTHING was my fault!

Linda - Emotionally abusive. He belittled me physically and mentally – belittled my clothing, my appearance, my hobbies, my interests, my career, etc.

Grace - Yes! Once I was away from him, and able to think clearly, I realized there was a LOT of abuse in the marriage! These issues were:

* Extreme control issues such as spying on me while bathing or showering, and absolute disrespect of my privacy when using the bathroom, etc. He kept me isolated, things like not allowing me to have my hair done or getting manicures or massages, despite having the income to support such luxuries. I was not allowed to shop outside of Christmas time and I had to ask permission to even buy groceries! His sons were his world, and I was an outsider. This encouraged a lack of respect in the boys, who, incidentally, were also immersed in pornography and showed huge outward signs of disrespect to me. It was like living in a private men's club!

- Financial abuse, going as far as having other bank accounts that, although he had both our names on them, I had no idea about. I have an incredible job with a professional income, but he insisted that I be on an "allowance" which I received when my sons received theirs. I was responsible for giving all receipts to him, but he had no joint responsibility in sharing any of our financial information with me. In fact, he was secretive about the amount of money coming into the home with our combined income.
- Sexual abuse. He was into sodomy and sodomizing himself. He had a fascination with paraphernalia, such as using dildos on himself and me. He dressed up in "masculine lingerie." On one occasion, he even exposed himself to me, aroused in my lingerie, asking if it "turned me on." This is called transvestite fetishism, and although these men can be heterosexual, this kind of activity is often a prelude to gay men coming out.
- Physical abuse. which included shoving me around and throwing things at me directly or indirectly. He also used intimidation through rage. He terrorized me by driving into oncoming traffic and displaying extreme episodes of road rage. Often these things happened when we were traveling alone, or out for a day by ourselves, but on occasion our children were with us. All these bouts of anger came out of nowhere.

Connie - He was not emotionally abusive until after I confronted him. It was like living with Satan himself. I was afraid of him. He intimidated me and made me feel like I was not a good person. He made me feel like I was nothing. He was very mean to me. I was very depressed all the time.

7. **Do you have children? If so, how many, what gender, and what are their current ages?**
   Gretchen - I have two children, a son who is 9 and a daughter who is 8.

Becky - I have two children. My daughter is currently 13; she was five when her dad moved out. My son is 10; he was three when his dad moved out of the house.

Linda - I have two sons, 25 and 21.

Grace - I have two natural sons; the eldest is 24 and married. The youngest is 21 and is living out of the country presently. I also care for two young ladies who are profoundly handicapped and medically fragile. These children have been in my care for many years.

Connie - I have three boys, ages 10, 9, and 8.

8. **Do your children know about your husband's homosexuality? If so, how does it affect them?**

Gretchen - My ex and I have never directly discussed his homosexuality with them. I believe that they have to understand what sex is before they can understand the different kinds. I do believe they have a cursory understanding of what "gay" is... my daughter briefly saw an HBO show I was watching in which two men where kissing. She asked me if those were two men; I said yes. She said, "Oh, then they're gay" in a very matter-of-fact tone. I said, "Yes, some men are gay" but I didn't elaborate and she didn't ask any more questions. I certainly will be open with my children about any questions having to do with sex, but at the moment, I feel there's no rush to give them more information than they want to know.

Becky - It has been seven years since he left and my kids were told August of this year (2004). My son was told by his father and my daughter had to hear it from me. My son had started to ask his dad questions about whether "he" (my son) was gay if his dad was gay. So at a later date, due to his (ex's) psychologist's encouragement, my ex brought up the subject with our son. Of course, our son didn't have much to say or ask him about, and his dad didn't push the conversation to encourage any questions or allow any feelings to be expressed. Instead, my son unleashed tons of emotions and questions on me. Then, because my daughter overheard the conversation my son and I were having, I had to tell her what we were talking about. I found out then that her dad had not included her in the conversation. The floodgates of emotions were REALLY released. She keeps them bottled up inside and is not confrontational. There was a lot of anger from both but especially my daughter. Of course, she had never discussed this with her dad personally and I don't think unless he brings it up, she will. I have informed him of what happened after he left and the pile of poop he left for me to pick up after.

Linda - Yes, he came out to them about two months after we separated. Both boys were in shock for three months. The younger one, Frank, moved in with his dad about three months after we separated and lived with him for the next five years. He and his dad live in Santa Fe and have a good father-son relationship. They have dinner together about once a month and talk on the phone several times a week.

In June, 2004, Frank and I talked a long time about how the breakup of our family had affected him. It took us five years to be able to have this conversation. Before this, he would talk a little, but was clearly uncomfortable and not able to discuss his thoughts and feelings. He told me how he hated that our family was torn apart, but that he truly understood that it was inevitable given his dad's sexuality.

Our older son, George, was very angry with his dad and did not speak to him for the first three years. About a year after our divorce, he wrote his dad a letter explaining that he still loved him, but that he was still too angry with him to talk with him. Since then, their relationship has healed somewhat, although they do not see each other often because they live 2000 miles apart.

George went off to college three months after my ex and I separated. He said he thinks that helped him survive the heartbreak and turmoil of the first years of our divorce. "One part of me was depressed about what was happening with my family, but at the same time, I was excited about my new life at college, so I immersed myself in school and campus activities."

Today he says he's no longer angry with his dad, but he just doesn't have much to do with him due to living so far apart. They talk on the phone about once every six months.

Grace - My sons are not aware that I believe their father is a gay man. I have kept silent about a lot of the issues that broke the marriage apart, aside from the homosexuality, as I don't believe they need to hear these things about their father. I understand that in remaining silent, I allow him to continue living a lie.

Connie - I think they know, but I'm not really sure. I have been afraid to tell them, but I know I will have to tell them one day. I do believe the boys recognize his girly ways (soft voice, loose wrist, twisty walk). They are getting older and I know they see that their father is different.

9. How did you meet your current husband/relationship?

Gretchen - My current husband and I met at a business conference where we had a client in common. He's from Canada and is very much into hockey (what a surprise!) I am an avid hockey fan, so we exchanged casual emails about my team who won the Stanley Cup that year. We then started to talk about our divorces, which he was going through at the same time. You can say we had a real Internet romance!

Becky - Actually we met on the computer.

Linda - Steve and I met via the Internet.

Grace - We met at a local hospital, where I was picking up medical supplies for one of the children in my care.

Connie - My sister's husband's aunt is engaged to my new love's brother. My sister called and asked her husband's aunt did her fiancé have a brother just like him? She said yes, and that he was coming to their house for Christmas. My sister told me about him and his brother told him about me. We met at the Christmas Eve party.

10. How long have you been together?

Gretchen - We met in early 2001 and were married (eloped, actually) in February, 2003 at an inn in Estes Park, Colorado, on a beautiful snowy day with the Rocky Mountains as a backdrop.

Becky - It has been two-and-a-half years since we met.

Linda - We've been seeing each other for three years. We plan to marry February 14, 2005.

Grace - Almost a year now!

Connie - Since Christmas Eve, 2003.

11. How does this relationship differ from the one with your gay husband?

Gretchen - HA! Actually, my ex- and my current husbands are creepily similar; they're both 6' 2", are absolutely blind without glasses and are left handed! But believe me, that's where the similarities end. I have true love in my current marriage. I have a man who believes in me, who trusts me, who thinks I am attractive, to whom I can turn when I'm worried or sad, who supports me, who understands my jokes, who loves sports, who doesn't care if the dishes didn't get done right after dinner.... on and on and on! Oh, did I mention sex?? I can say without hesitation that no one ever made love to me until I met this wonderful man!

Becky - The most important difference is our communication and my comfort level with talking to him about all kinds of things, the good and the bad.

Linda - Both Steve and I believe in radical honesty and we each make a more conscious effort to do loving things for each other. We are also more appreciative of each other. Sexually, I perceive a difference in the nature of his desire. Sexually, he does not have the control and stamina my ex did, but he pleases me generously in other ways.

Grace - This man is incredibly respectful of me in every manner. We share an intimacy that I never had in my marriage, in every form, emotional, physical and sexual.

Connie - When I was with my gay husband, I felt empty. I didn't feel loved desired or respected. I felt like I was in a cold cave doomed to live there the rest of my life. Every day I wanted to die, because I didn't want to face another day of pain. I was so unhappy. I was miserable. With my new love, I am always smiling. He makes me laugh. I love who I am when I'm with him. He loves me unconditionally. He makes me feel beautiful. He has helped me become the woman that I was before the gay husband/straight wife marriage. I am strong and confident. I have my self-esteem back. I am a whole woman again. Sometimes after we make love and he is holding me, I close my eyes and say a prayer, "thank you, God, for this man." I am totally happy.

12. Did it take you a long time to gain back your sense of trust in your new relationship due to the problems in your last one?

Gretchen - When I first began to realize that divorce was inevitable and that I would be single again, I resigned myself to living alone for the rest of my life (which was preferable to living with my ex!) Given how hard it was to find my first husband and how much older and less attractive I thought I was, and two children to boot, I didn't think I'd ever find anyone. Nevertheless, as my friendship with my current husband blossomed into something deeper, all my concerns became irrelevant. One of the things that I love so much about him is how he fosters trust, not just in me, but also in us. When he says he loves me, there is nothing in the world that makes me think otherwise. I never, ever felt this way with my ex-husband. I cherish every moment with my new husband.

Becky - Amazingly, I was surprised, but no, it didn't. I guess the comfort level of our relationship must have ruled over any thoughts of insecurity. It was also two years after my divorce was final, so I think I had gotten my head together and had gotten past some of my insecurities.

Linda - Yes. At times, I still feel unlovable, nerdy and unfeminine.

Grace - Yes, I had zero self-esteem and no trust when I first met him. It has been a battle for me to be able to make myself vulnerable and open to him. But he is SO patient with me, and has not faltered one bit along the journey!

Connie - Yes, a little at first. I was very scared. I was an emotional wreck. But my new love never gave up on me. I put him through a lot of emotional drama. He could have walked away, but he told me I was worth fighting for.

13. **Do you have any regrets about ending your marriage to your gay husband?**
Gretchen - Only that it didn't happen sooner! I will say, however, that I don't regret getting married to him, even knowing what I know now, because of the two beautiful children that were the product of our marriage. Not every moment of our marriage was horrible and I started out with so much hope that my dreams of "happily ever after" were being fulfilled. I'm also aware that this experience has made me a stronger person and taught me things about what I'm capable of.
Becky - NO NO NO and No again!!
Linda - I have no regrets about ending my marriage of 29 years; however, I feel deep sorrow. My ex and I had a cosmic rapport from the time we first met at age 10. We share 29 years worth of experiences and memories, many good ones. We ran a couple of businesses together and had many mutual interests – we were hard-core gardeners, musicians and artists. I am still passionately interested in these things today and often miss the "good old days" when we talked, plotted and planned our projects, gigs, etc.
Grace - I have no regrets. I have gained myself back. I do have a deep sadness about the loss of years, and the loss of myself during those years. Oddly enough, I only feel pity now for him. I do not believe for one moment that he wants to be this way. It goes against all his religious beliefs and upbringing.
Connie - No... No...No (excuse my French) HELL NO!!!!

14. **Have your children adjusted/accepted the new man in your life?**
Gretchen - My children have adjusted incredibly well, primarily because they were at a good age to accept changes in their lives (they were 6 and 7 when their father and I divorced). They do very well in school and socially and don't complain

about living in two different households. My current husband pointed out very accurately that it was so much better for them to have the example of marriage where their mother is shown respect and love, than to remain with their father who showed neither, even if it means that their parents are divorced. My current husband is very careful to respect the boundaries and not to interfere with the decisions that only the children's father should be involved with, yet he is such a good "buddy" to my children, playing with them, teaching them sports that their father has no interest in. It is very obvious that my children love their stepfather and he loves them.

Becky - They have really been supportive of the relationship. They really miss him when he isn't around. My son wanted to know if he could call him "Dad."

Linda - My sons like and respect Steve. They have a number of interests in common. Steve has been extremely kind and generous to my older son who lives nearby. My son has gone out of his way to do favors for Steve. Both boys have told me they know I could not stay married to a gay man and that they want me to find a new husband who is right for me.

Grace - My eldest son is still angry. He does not understand the depths that I went through with his father, and is at this point, unwilling to talk about it all. He is polite around the new man in my life.

My youngest son lived through a lot more with me, and he has been supportive of me since I asked his father to leave. He does not speak a lot of what happened, but is very aware of the abuse in the marriage, and asked that I not go back into it. He is also very aware of how differently the new man in my life treats me, and has spoken directly to me about this.

Connie - At first, my oldest son had major problems with me having a boyfriend. I had to continue to tell him that his father and I were never ever getting back together. He then started to accept it better. He saw how happy my boyfriend made me and I think that helped a lot. When they first saw me and my new love hugging, they looked in amazement because they never saw me and their father give each other a hug, kiss or anything! Now the boys think he is so cool. They want to be just like him. They tell me how much they love him and what a good person he is, all the time. One day my new love was laying on the couch napping. My middle son went over to him and asked him was he OK and told him he loved him. It made my new love cry.

15. Did it take time to rebuild your sense of self and sexual esteem after your marriage?
Gretchen - I was so lucky to have found someone new right away who built me up so much by his loving attention. In retrospect, I really had been affected by my ex-husband's constant criticism, even though I've always thought of myself as a confident and able woman. It wore me down and I began to believe that I wasn't attractive and capable. My current husband is the most wonderful sexual partner a woman could have, but he was very sensitive to my situation and took things slowly... at first! He jokes that he'd like to thank my ex for giving him a wife who, after years of repressed desire, is making up for lost time!
Becky - Yes, it took lots of time and understanding that it wasn't about me. I was angry for a long time and figured out it was OK to be angry. I am not good at being angry. I had several friends who were going through divorce at the same time but of course it was so different because a heterosexual affair brought on their divorce. We had things in common but then so much was different. Not until I realized it was OK to take care of ME and make ME a priority did I start to move past the anger and forward. Then, of course, finding support through Bonnie and the AOL online message board did I realize I wasn't crazy. It is amazing how many things are similar and how our gay husbands have the same ways of behaving. It was very comforting to find. I so appreciate everything Bonnie does and has done for me and the rest of us in this situation. It can be very isolating because of society not accepting the gay lifestyle. Bonnie helped me feel less isolated and I appreciate that.
Linda - Yes, about three years.

Grace - Yes, it did and it that continues to be an area that I have to constantly work on in my life.

Connie - Yes, I was very uncomfortable because my ex always made me feel like I was undesirable and told me no one would ever want me because I was fat and ugly. I thought I was going to be treated the same way from my new love. It took a long time for me to be intimate with him. When we first made love, it was so wonderful! He desired me, he had passion for me, he made love to my mind, body and soul! Did I say it was **wonderful**? (BIG smile!)

16. **What words of encouragement would you give to other women who are struggling with life after gay husband?**

Gretchen - I believe the most valuable lesson I learned is to have confidence in your ability to persevere, especially since so many women in this situation have been put down to a great extent and have lost so much self-esteem. You can be paralyzed by such behavior, and you have to believe that you can change your situation. There are many hard things to overcome, but believe in yourself and you can do anything and make your life better! Also remember that you're not alone; more and more women are confronting this situation and finding support through organizations such as Bonnie's. It was my greatest source of comfort in a world that just didn't understand what it is like to be us.

Becky - First and foremost, know that it is not YOU that is the problem or the cause, no matter what your gay husband has told you in the past. Reach out and find support through whatever means you can. Find someone to talk to, hopefully in person also. The personal touch and support is important. Get your feelings out, talking, writing, drawing whatever it takes. Take care of YOURSELF first. It took me a long time to figure out that it didn't do my kids any favors if I didn't take care myself. They needed me to be strong and healthy physically and emotionally. Someone said to me or I read it somewhere, that if I didn't take care of myself, who would? My ex sure didn't spend anytime worrying about me or what was in my best interest.

Another HUGE turning point for me was realizing that I was a role model for my children and what they would grow to think healthy relationships were. Would I want my daughter to grow up thinking that it was OK for the person she loved to put her down and lie to her? Would I want my son to grow up thinking that he could yell and scream, put down and be unfaithful to the person he chose to spend his life with? So if I put up with those things, they would grow up to think that maybe they should also.

There is the issue of distancing yourself from your gay husband so that you can learn to let go and heal. There is a great post that circulated on the AOL support message board about distancing, about only having conversations that you HAVE to (about the children, the divorce, business stuff). You don't need to hear stories about his life, let him cry on your shoulder or do things to help him, or be his cheerleader. He lost that right when he chose to cheat, lie and take on secrets from you. It took me almost a year to figure that difficult lesson out also. You cannot move on when you are so intertwined and know everything, good and bad, that is going on in his life.

That old saying that "time heals wounds" is absolutely a killer but it is so true. Just give yourself time. Take baby steps, don't expect big things from yourself or anyone else. Take up old hobbies you let fall behind, find some new ones. Keep in touch with friends, look up old ones you have lost touch with and find new friends. Keep yourself out there through church, community, and school whatever it might be. Exercise, take long soaking baths, read a new book. When you are right with yourself you will find you will draw up positive people around you, and you will find all kinds of avenues for new relationships to be in. Live life and love it!

Linda - Make time to get to know yourself. Read self-help books, participate in a support group, get massage therapy, and find a couple of close friends you can really talk with about your situation.

In the first months after he came out and we separated, the technique that helped me most was to focus on "right here, right now." I found that if I concentrated all my energy on what

I was doing – driving my car along the highway, walking through a park, fixing dinner, working, or whatever – that I would not think about my husband and our separation. I would ask myself what difference all my heartbreak and turmoil had to do with what I was doing right at that moment, and usually, it had nothing to do with what I was doing. I gave myself a certain time each day to think about my marital situation and to cry.

Grace - There is life after these marriages! Don't lose hope! Take time to heal on the inside. Focus on your children and on those things that are important to you! Get yourself STRONG!

Connie - There is a pot of gold at the end of the rainbow, just don't give up. It will be hard and some days will be tough. There were times when I wanted to give up, but just being out of the same house with "TGO" (the gay one) was a relief to me. Just never give up and don't ever look back. Keep going forward. Leaving the marriage is the hardest part. Once you leave, you are on your journey to recovery. **You can survive. You will survive**.

CHAPTER 11

SIGNS OF CHEATING CHECKLIST

When you suspect that your husband is gay and it is a constant nagging feeling...you are in almost all cases correct. Most women see signs through changes in their husbands' behaviors or characteristics. It's funny how these behaviors lead women to believe that it's a gay sexual issue versus a cheating with a woman issue. I tell women TRUST YOUR INSTINCTS. In 98% of all of the cases, their instincts prove to be right.

In a survey that was done by a married gay men's organization in the UK, nearly 300 gay married who were still living secret lives were surveyed. The results were devastating for straight wives. They revealed that 13% of the husbands planned to tell their wives one day, 32% of the husbands stated that they would NEVER tell their wives, and over 50% didn't know if they would ever tell their wives. Those are pretty scary numbers. Realistically, I say that over 60% of women will never have the "confession" they are looking for which really plays havoc on their emotional state.

It never stops amazing me that wives of gay husbands need some extra validation of their husbands' homosexuality before they feel they can move on in their lives. They spend their days looking for hints or clues to the crime, on one hand wanting to learn the truth, but in other cases, looking to evidence that will allay their suspicions. The funny thing is that even when they find the proof, it's never ENOUGH proof. So many women repeat the same line to me: Am I going to break up my marriage just because I found some calls to a gay chatroom? Do I walk away from a marriage because I found gay porno? These women need more proof. The fact that their husbands don't touch them in bed or want to make love to them isn't enough proof. The fact that are looking at gay porno on the Internet isn't enough proof—after all, their husbands claim to be bored—curious—into any porno even though it's only gay popping up.

I tell my women to stop spending your life being a detective. There is nothing more debilitating than to spend your valuable time investigating your husband. I did it for several years—checking his pockets, his notes, his papers, listening to his phone calls from the other side of the wall with a glass—you name it, I tried it. Why did I keep obsessing over this? I needed to know that my suspicions were more than my imagination. So when I thought I had concrete proof and I confronted him, he went into a rage telling me that I was crazy. And guess what? I was relieved because I WANTED TO BELIEVE. And please don't tell me that I was stupid because I know the majority of you out there want to believe as much as I do that this nightmare is anything but what it is. You don't have to confront your husband—you just have to know the truth for yourself. That should be enough. And when you do know the truth, then you need to set yourself free, because living with a gay man can never fulfill your expectations of what you want out of life. No way. Ever.

But for those of you who are ready to make an honest attempt at unraveling the signs of cheating, here are some of the signs that you should be looking for:

1. **If you see a sudden change in appearance through exercise, clothing, haircuts, and colognes and a decline in his attention to you, this is a sign.**

    When your husband is attracted to or involved with another man, you will often see him transform within weeks by reshaping his looks. You may have told him for years that he is overweight, but he didn't notice or care. But now he's running to the gym—and not just running, but exercising with a vengeance. When he goes out, he gets dressed up, looks good, and smells sexy. When he comes home to you, he doesn't care if he looks unkempt, unshaved, and unbathed. He now goes to get his hair "styled" and may even have a pierced ear or tattoo. These are definitely tell-tale signs that his interests in men are now on the upswing, and he has met someone or is about to meet someone to have an encounter or relationship with.

2. **If you notice a changes in sexual activity—decrease or increase—and change in sexual habits, this is a sign. Some women ask me why increasing sexual activity would be a sign. Often, if a man feels guilty for cheating on you or afraid that you will suspect he is going elsewhere. He goes out of his way to pump up the action to relieve your suspicions and fears.**

Some gay men have semi-normal sexual activity with their wives at least during their 20's and 30's. Most of the time it declines early in the relationship, but there is a small percentage of men who continue sexual relations. If a man suddenly stops having sex, chances are he's found another man to have it with. He'll come up with the usual excuses of being too tired, too overworked, too stressed out, unable to perform due to medication, too depressed, too pressured and so on. But the reality is he's having great sex with a man and doesn't want you.

Then you have the exact reverse of what I call the "honeymoon period." I wrote this column in my newsletter a number of years ago:

THE HONEYMOON REVISITED

I love happy endings to stories. With straight/gay marriages, some of you also have the advantage of having some happy middles of stories even if the endings are sad. Of course, these middle stories don't last very long, but while they happen, it's like having a second honeymoon.

I hear it from many women. The story is usually the same, so here goes a typical one that I received this week:

Dear Bonnie,
It's a miracle! After I confronted my husband with my suspicions about his being gay, he admitted to me that he had passing thoughts about men but would never act on them. And now, things are better than they've ever been. Now it's just like when we were on our honeymoon—but even better. My husband is being very attentive to me and very

considerate. For the first time in years, he is being affectionate to me. He is holding my hand in public and kissing me goodnight every night.

And now for the best part—my husband realizes that he is not gay.

He has approached me for sex for the first time in years. He is really doing everything to be the kind of husband that I knew he could be if he could just get those homosexual thoughts out of his head. Now I realize that we can move forward in our marriage with all of the bad times behind us."

Most of the time, the letters end with, "You were wrong, Bonnie." Sometimes, I'll hear a more insightful thought from a woman saying, "I know that this is just a temporary stage, but I'll take it for the moment!"

I do want to tell you that these honeymoons don't last for long. Sometimes they'll last a few weeks or even a few months. But as letters that come in later with humble apologies to me say, the "honeymoon revisited phase" is usually over within a short amount of time. You see, after the husbands lulls you into a false sense of security once again, he feels he has you back where he wants you and so his "Normal," or shall we say, "Abnormal," patterns creep back slowly, or sometimes quickly. But they always come back. I tell these women there is no need to apologize. I know how I used to hang on to any false hope that came my way no matter how quickly it whizzed past my eyes.

Why do our gay husbands revisit the honeymoon phase? Quite simple. They fear that you now suspect or know the truth about their homosexuality and they are determined to throw you off track and start doubting yourself. They are not ready to be honest, and so they buy time. They become affectionate, attentive, and start to give you unexpected gifts. They say they are willing to work on their "sexual dysfunction." The claim they will go for marriage counseling, and in some cases, give it a try for a few weeks or months.

And you feel good. You start believing that your suspicion about the worst possible scenario is untrue. And all those little signs that you thought were leading you in that direction were really something else. Maybe it was just a curiosity phase. Maybe your husband was having problems from medications. Maybe he does have some gay tendencies, but maybe that's from an extra chromosome or two that has been misplaced. Maybe he's learned his lesson by realizing that you are going to leave your marriage if you find out that he's doing his thing.

Then you think you are so "stupid" when the second honeymoon is over and reality hits again. Please don't apologize or feel stupid. I was lulled endless times into what I wanted to be a functioning marriage. I grasped for any sign of rebuttal from my husband and swore I could make things better if only he would work with me on it. Yes, I even had a couple of extra sexual encounters that *he* initiated in good faith to prove to me that our marriage would be A-okay. But how long could he fool me? He couldn't even fool himself. He couldn't carry out this lie indefinitely, and within a short time, things reverted to where they were—or shall I say deteriorated back to where they were—when I threw out my suspicions.

So, next time you see things changing, be aware that it is just a temporary ploy. Don't get your hopes up—enjoy the peace and quiet for whatever time it lasts. Use this time to strengthen yourself mentally because this is not the time that your husband will be battering you down mentally. Recognize it for what it is and take advantage of the quiet time to make a plan to protect yourself and your future. And rest assured—the honeymoon will be over before you know it. Once you understand this, your chances of being disappointed will become one of expectation and much easier to handle.

* * * * *

3. **Watch out for unusual computer habits of spending much too much time on the Internet, opening up email accounts or not wanting you to be around when he's on the computer. Also, watch to see if sleep patterns change because he could be going into chatrooms late at night while you are sleeping. I know men who have online relationships for hours each night while their wives sleep.**

This has become one of the easiest ways of learning the truth about—or shall I say *catching* your gay husband. First, if he has a separate password from you, that means he has something to hide from you if he won't reveal it. To me, this means there's a problem already. There shouldn't have to be secrets so big in a relationship that your spouse doesn't allow you to know about.

Many of these men become addicted to the computer for (1) porn, (2) chatrooms, or (3) gay websites. They will spend hours locked in a room with the computer convincing you that they are doing work. Trust me, no one is working that hard in a locked room hour after hour, day after day. A large number of these men are also masturbating to gay porn or cybersex which is also why the door is locked. I know that this is upsetting to hear this, but you need to face the reality.

If you have any doubts about what your husband is doing, you can invest $99.00 and order spyware. Spyware records every note he is typing and will tell you his password, instant messages, chatrooms, emails, and websites. There will be no way for your husband to detect it, and you can access the information from any computer anywhere after you download the program. Many of my women use this link to order the spyware:

http://www.spectorsoft.com/default.asp?affil=1893

Just type that link into your browser and you're moments away from getting the information you are desperately trying to prove. Remember—you have to be emotionally ready to accept what you find. It will be painful, nauseating, and emotionally overwhelming. But as they say—the truth will set you free.

4. **If your man starts to find fault with you even though you are doing nothing differently, this is a sign. Criticizing you is a way for him to ease his guilt.**

My gay ex-husband friend Jay wrote these hard-hitting words for my newsletters a number of years ago. The words still ring true in my head:

I was much more demanding about the order around me when I was married to my ex-wife. While I still like a nice home, I find I am less compulsive about cleaning and demanding that those around me keep things tidy and neat. I believe that my need for external order in my prior life was a way of coping with my own internal chaos (and tension created by my attempts to compartmentalize my being.) Of course, my discomfort with disorder at home also served to legitimize my disappointment in my ex-wife as a homemaker. "If only she were a better wife.......we would be happy" was my mantra. Indeed, she was disorganized and sloppy, but as it turned out, I have realized that IF ONLY SHE HAD BEEN A MAN, I WOULD HAVE BEEN MORE TOLERANT. Ouch.

Jay explained this frustration honestly from the point of view of a gay husband. So many other gay husbands have expressed this to me. Why do they do this? Simple. They have to have SOMETHING to control in their marriages, and they can't control their sexuality no matter how much they try. Keeping a "clean house" gives the illusion of control.

A number of my women also state that their husbands are "controlling." They like to control the family bank accounts, credit cards, where you live, shopping, vacations, places to eat, movies you go to and anything else they can. Once again, since they have no control in their sexuality, they try to control the outside environment—and you. This is definitely a form of emotional abuse when you don't have a say in what is going on in the marriage.

5. **If he's constantly checking on your schedule and what time you're doing things, this is a sign. Cheating men try to plan their activities—liaisons, phone calls, dinners, etc. around times that you will not be around.**

   Many ex-husbands like to have information about YOUR free time habits even though they aren't telling you anything about theirs. If your husband keeps asking you where you're going, who you're going with, and when you're coming home, don't assume it's because he's missing you. He's making his own plans and wants to make sure they are coordinated with yours to avoid suspicion.

6. **Some men change their working habits, working late or going out of town on trips too often.**

   There are an extraordinary number of women who have husbands whose work habits change once they start "stepping out" in the gay world. All of a sudden, their bosses are sending them away on trips. Or if they own businesses, they are looking to expand business or find new contacts that require a night or two away from home. Those men who work at home who are now locked in their home offices until late hours are either in chatrooms, viewing online pornography, or answering ads for gay hookups.

7. **If he has a sudden lack of affection, this could be a sign. The less affection he shows, the more likely he is getting it somewhere else.**

   Even though a number of gay husbands don't want to have sex with their wives, they do show affection because they love their wives. They will hold hands, peck the cheek or the lip, cuddle in bed, hold their wives while they are sleeping, and give the "illusion" that they are perfectly happy and satisfied through being affectionate.

   When these women tell me that they are devastate because their husbands no longer want to cuddle or be close, this means they have someone else they want to be close with. This is definitely a sure sign. Usually your husband has fallen deeply for another man who can satisfy him totally—not just with a peck on the lips. Once he feels passion for the man, his affection for you will quickly diminish.

8. **If he begins listening to different types of music, he didn't like before, it may be because that is the music choice of his "new lover".**

    If you see your husband develop new interests or tastes that are outside of what you think his realm could ever be, it's something to start worrying about. Often when our husbands fall in love or lust with another man, the feelings are so strong that they adapt to the things that please their new partners. Men who never cared about classical music before are now listening to Chopin or Mozart. And watch out when he wants to watch movies like Brokeback Mountain. His taste in movies may also take a sudden change.

9. **Pay close attention to smell. If he smells like smoke or cologne, and you don't smoke and he doesn't wear that cologne, he is with someone else who does.**

    This is a definite give away. The smoke is usually explained away by being in a bar with co-workers and smokers. But the cologne? If he smells like someone else, he's been with someone else.

10. **If you are getting too many wrong numbers or hang ups on your home phone, this can be a sign that someone is calling your house who shouldn't be.**

    Women who catch their husbands have commented to me that a number of them were tipped off by repeated wrong numbers when their husbands were home or hang-ups at strange times of the night. It certainly gave them an extra reason to feel suspicious, and added together with all the other signs, pushed them to seek out cell phone bills when they could get a copy to look for a pattern. I've had women call these secret lovers of their husbands and confront them on the phone. That always makes for interesting conversation the next day!

11. **Money habits such as too many withdrawals from the bank account or opening up a separate account can be a sure sign.**

Many of our women knew something was wrong when the finances of their life were falling apart. Their husbands couldn't explain why bills weren't being paid or where the money was going. This isn't always easy since a lot of the men want to control the family money in order to have some control in their lives from the beginning. However, that being said, a woman can often tell if her husband is overspending. One way is to get a hold of the bank and credit card statements and see where the payments have been going. If you see purchases for unaccounted for dinners, hotel rooms, shows, movies, or items that are not showing up in your house, that's a good place to start.

12. **Communication is the key to all relationships, so if you find that he used to talk to you about anything and everything, but now he doesn't, this could be a problem. If he avoids you around the house, secludes himself in other rooms, or is more irritable when asked of simple questions, cheating could be the reason why.**

When your husband has nothing to say to you or the communication seems like it has faded, it's often because he's communicating so much better with a new side lover. He doesn't feel like having his "talkative" wife babbling sweet nothings when he's thinking about a man who can intellectually stimulate him just by talking about the weather. It doesn't matter how much you know or how smart you are. Once he meets Mr. Right, you'll always be wrong in what you have to say.

Now that I've gone through some of the possible alerts, here are things you can do for checking them out.

HOW TO CHECK FOR CHEATING

✓ Go through his wallet and clothes for receipts, match books, and phone numbers. Men get careless and leave clues behind.

✓ Check ATM receipts for time and date. This could help determine if your man was out when he claimed to be working. If your man withdraws from a bank branch, the location is usually printed on there. This could help tell where he was at what time.

✓ If he says he is working overtime, make sure to check his paycheck and look for overtime hours and match the dates.

✓ Check your credit card statements very carefully for signs of dinners out, motels or hotels and even car rentals.

✓ Look through your partner's mobile phone book, missed calls, outgoing and received calls. If he is hiding his phone from you, that is a problem.

✓ Check the mileage on his car. You know how far he should be driving for work, and anything above or below that could be a tell-tale sign.

✓ Tracking devises for the car reveal all of the movements of your husband letting you know where he is going.

✓ Check the condom supplies. If you see that they are missing, time to find out why if you know they are not missing at the rate you are having sex.

The most important key to catching your husband cheating is to act like you are completely oblivious to the fact something is wrong. He will let his guard down and then you can follow him or keep checking for evidence.

<u>TIPS ON WHAT TO DO WHEN YOU KNOW</u>

If you start gathering evidence against your man, DO NOT CONFRONT HIM immediately, but rather gather the evidence that you will need when you confront him and for use it in case you have to take legal action. I know how difficult this is for some women. You finally have CAUGHT HIM and you want to let him know he can't make a fool of you any longer. This is a BAD MOVE. Once you tell him you caught him, he'll have time to remove any evidence he has around the house including his computer hard-drive. He'll also be alerted and be much more careful not to slip up in the future. It will take a long time until he makes his next mistake knowing that you're watching him. He'll also make sure to go through that "honeymoon phase" with you just to throw you off track and buy more time. Don't get trapped in that trap!

Be smart and accumulate as much evidence as you can and make copies of everything. Store it safely away OUTSIDE of your home. If you don't have family or friends where you can leave it, invest in a safe deposit box so that it will be secure.

Next, consult a good attorney to check your legal rights. Every state has different laws and rights. Know what yours are before you drop the information. You've invested lots of time, energy, and emotional well-being into your fraudulent marriage. You want to make sure to come out as much as a winner under these losing circumstances.

End the relationship because there's no sense putting yourself through the emotional turmoil that you'll face forever in your marriage. Learn to accept your husband is gay, and no matter how hard you try to change that, you can't. No amount of therapy, plastic surgery, dieting, or kindness can rearrange those genetics in his body. You can waste years of your valuable life trying to make a square peg fit in a round hole, but in time, you'll realize that no matter how hard you keep hammering it, the hole is still round and can't change.

Look for support groups that can help you through the process. It is so difficult dealing with this alone. You feel isolated and vulnerable. Many organizations offer online support groups or in-person ones. I offer online support three times a week for people who are ready or getting ready to move on in their lives. Although you feel isolated and alone, remember there are over 4 million women who have lived or who are living your life. Just write to me at **Bonkaye@aol.com** and I'll set you up with us.

CHAPTER 12

STARTING OVER

As a postscript, I want to leave you, the reader, with a strong sense of hope and optimism. Not a false sense, but a genuine feeling that life will move ahead when you allow it to do so. I love hearing from women whose lives I have touched over the years who found real happiness the next time around when they met the mates they needed and deserved. Of course, not all of the stories had a "happily ever after" ending. Those women who didn't learn from the mistakes of their marriages to their gay husbands often found themselves in the wrong relationships again under different circumstances. This is why it is so important to realize that you need the time to rebuild yourself and find happiness within yourself without depending on someone else to make you feel worthy.

I took the time I needed to do this, and the investment paid off. Excusing the use of a cliché, I "followed my dreams" by returning to school and earned my degrees in counseling. I raised my children as a single parent facing the challenges of juggling work, family, friends, and personal time alone. I made plenty of mistakes along the way, but I tried to learn from each one of them so I wouldn't repeat them. I learned to trust and love again, but that was after I felt whole as a person. I am still faced daily with new adversities to overcome, but I guess that's what makes you appreciate the good times in life that much more. I take nothing for granted—I look at each new day as an adventure in living.

When my marriage ended, I felt isolated and alone. There was virtually nowhere to turn, so I started my own support group. As I mentioned earlier, I started the support group to be just that—a group that would support people in straight/gay marriages regardless of the status of the marriage. As time went on, that changed when I saw how self-defeating these marriages were for the wives who existed in a state of acceptance for their husbands' needs. In good conscience, I was unable to support couples who wanted to stay together and work it out. Since neither partner could ever be really happy, it was a lose-lose situation. What's the point in advocating a losing situation?

Over the years, some women who were angered by my stance have come back to me and told me that I was right—there was no way the marriages could work. I didn't feel any sense of happiness in their admitted defeat. I am never one to say, "I told you so," because who am I to judge the rate of acceptance that it takes someone to realize they are trapped in their own insecurities, if ever.

Each of us has to find the way out of this tangled maze at her own pace. Each of us has be able to have the strength to move ahead, making our own timetable and not being influenced by the outside pressures that so often get in the way. These pressures can be from family, religious beliefs, well-meaning friends, counselors, or the misguided advice from some support groups that make you feel that if you can't keep the marriage together, you are the failure.

When looking for support in this area, there are places to turn. How do you start to find the proper resources? My most important message to you before starting this search is to remember that there are groups all over this country that may not meet your needs. If this is the case, retreat immediately—don't become more confused by a message that is uncomfortable to you. Keep looking and if you still can't find the help you are looking for, consider starting your own group that will work for you.

I am happy to share my thoughts and input with those of you who need help and guidance through email or my online support group. Feel free to write to me for support, information, and my monthly newsletter, or to join my chatroom.

My email address is: **Bonkaye@aol.com.**

CHAPTER 13

BONNIE'S STRAIGHT TALK COLUMNS

Since 2001, I have been writing monthly newsletters for my support base of over 7,000 women around the world. Each month, I explain different aspects of marriages to gay husbands and how they impact our lives. In September 2008, these past newsletters will be compiled into a book of writings. Here are some of my favorite words from my earlier newsletters.

If you would like to purchase the full compilation of seven years of newsletters, look for it in September through CCB Publishing. If you would like to receive the free newsletters sent out monthly, please email me at **Bonkaye@aol.com** and I will be happy to add you to my mailing list.

April 2001

PROFOUND AND REVEALING WORDS
FROM A GAY EX-HUSBAND

I receive several letters each week from men who are struggling to come out to their wives. I respond quickly to these men in hopes that my support and encouragement will give them the courage to be honest with their spouses. I also receive several letters each month from gay men who find my website or see my book who commend me for the work I am doing in helping people understand the complexities of straight/gay marriages.

Two months ago, I received a letter from a man who was about to become an important part of my life. Jay is an attorney in Pennsylvania. He is the first man I have ever met who can write words in a manner that clarified all of my own thoughts and feelings allowing me to conceptualize a key to the problem of straight/gay marriages that I will share with you. Jay's sensitivity and honesty reflects what most of us would like our husbands or ex-husbands to tell us. Too few of us ever get to hear these words. I asked Jay if I could reprint some of his thoughts because I believe it validates so much of what all of us feel and need to hear. After reading his words, I am sure you will appreciate not only what he says, but also the beauty of how he says it.

Jay's first communication to me in early February stated:
I am a gay man who was married for 23 years. My ex-wife and I have two children. I am writing to encourage you to continue the important work you are doing. I only wish that in 1996 when I finally began to come out that there had been resources such as yours to support our family through our transition.

I thanked him for his kind words, and his response was this:
I think that both men and women in these circumstances must recognize that there are no winners but there are survivors who create new ways to relate, maintain, support and redefine their family. In the process of ending my marriage, I lost my best friend and the dream we had of growing old together. Slowly, we have worked to continue to parent our children in accordance with the many values that we continue to share. There are many things I would, in retrospect have done and handled differently, but my single largest regret is that I did not deal with the secret of my sexuality while still in my marriage and in the years of counseling before divorce. So to those men who you counsel , I would urge them to give the woman they chose to love and bear children the earliest chance to deal with the truth. They probably will not have a marriage together, but they will at least have a chance of preserving the love that once brought them together with hopes and plans for a lifetime.

More words of insight kept coming as the weeks progressed. I will highlight just a few of these pearls that will lead to my conclusion:

I keep reminding myself of the shame that fueled my own 'denial' and kept me closeted for most of my life, however I also know the damage that secrets do to those who keep them and would like to teach that lesson to my kids as well.

...my kids have always been a priority. I can recall vividly, my own frustration at seeking advice on how to come out to my kids and finding little support from the gay or straight communities. Of course, I was looking for the right way to do it and assure that the kids would not go off the deep end or reject me. No one could have given me the surefire approach. However, I think there is a real void. God knows there are self help books out there on everything else.

No woman deserves to be in this situation. In the past, I spent a lot of time searching my own soul, trying to figure out how much of the failure of my marriage was attributable to homosexuality and how much was the struggle for control, neediness and other dynamics extant in any couple relationship. My ex-wife and I hurt each other a lot. There are still things about her that I dislike, but I have concluded that the presence of my secret in that relationship was the primary poison. Much of the rest of our conflicts flowed from it....the absence of trust, the neediness, possessiveness, the anger and ultimately the conflict that I both created (even if it was not by premeditated design) and used to find the impetus despair and courage to leave. Accordingly, as painful as it is to admit, I know that the secret and immutability of my homosexuality is inextricably bound up in all that was wrong in our relationship. Yes, I had difficult issues to confront. As with any person facing difficult times, some of them I handled quite poorly. I could empathize with your own horror and dismay at how you thought and acted at various points.

I share your belief that bisexuality is often a transitional label and crutch used by homosexuals unable or unwilling to come to terms with their natural orientation. I lived that myself. After my separation from my wife, I woke one morning after a date with a woman and was appalled by the self discovery that I might do this to another woman because I hated who and how I was.

And the most profound words were yet to come:

I was much more demanding about the order around me when I was married to my ex-wife. While I still like a nice home, I find I am less compulsive about cleaning and demanding that those around me keep things tidy and neat. I believe that my need for external order in my prior life was a way of coping with my own internal chaos (and tension created by my attempts to compartmentalize my being.) Of course, my discomfort with disorder at home also served to legitimize my disappointment in my ex-wife as a homemaker. "If only she were a better wife...we would be happy" was my mantra. Indeed, she was disorganized and sloppy, but as it turned out, I have realized that IF ONLY SHE HAD BEEN A MAN, I WOULD HAVE BEEN MORE TOLERANT. Ouch.

All of Jay's words allowed me come to a great realization. For those of us who have or had gay husbands who complained actively or passively about our inadequacies and faults as wives, I have another thought:

Who would we be today if we had a straight husband? How would our destiny have changed if we were loved, nurtured, sexually desired with passion and tenderness, given emotional support and encouragement, and made to feel like we were part of a real couple in tune with each other's needs, wants, and aspirations? What if we didn't have to spend countless hours each day wondering why we were failures as wives, women, and lovers—ripping away our self-esteem layer by layer until we became strangers unto ourselves and others? What if our husbands' dishonesty and cheating didn't change us to become untrusting, suspicious, and doubting wives, forcing us to question our ability to make rational decisions? How many of us were sidetracked through those "detours of deceit" that diverted us from the direction that life might have taken otherwise?

Bottom line—no matter how much a gay man loves a straight woman, it is not the kind of love that fulfills the basic human need that all of us have. It can never be the kind of love that inspires the music that becomes classics or the poetry that makes the heart flutter. It is not the kind of love that can ever be returned to the degree that you are giving it. Even the best of relationships are barely more than great friendships—not the passion and excitement that make us thrive and look forward to waking up each day. And even these relationships are woven with dishonesty, distrust, infidelity, resentment, and frustration. Life was not meant to be this complicated.

What Jay has done for me personally is say what I am still waiting for my ex-husband to say after 20 years. Occasionally, a word of wisdom will float out from my ex-husband expressing how "screwed up" he was through the years. Does it change anything? Not really. But yes, knowing the truth does help validate who we are, what we became because of our gay husbands, and how we can change and now move forward. It's the first step towards healing the scars, bridging the understanding, and bringing closure to a chapter in our lives.

May 2001

GAMES PEOPLE PLAY – THE "IF ONLY" AND THE "BLAME" GAMES

I have worked with too many women who at first assume that the reason for their husbands' homosexuality is due to something they did wrong. For those of us who have had time to work through this problem over a longer period, it is easy for us to react by saying that this thinking is ludicrous. But try to remember when you first suspected or discovered your husband's interest in men. Then it doesn't seem quite as ridiculous.

When I reflect on my own inner feelings of shame during those early years, I remember feeling a great sense of responsibility. I used to play a game that most of us fall prey to. I call it the **"If Only Game."** It goes like this. "If only I could be a better wife....if only I was more attractive...if only I was better as a lover...if only I was a better housekeeper, if only I wasn't so demanding...if only I could lose more weight....if only I was smarter...if only, if only, if only...then maybe he could love me enough not to think of men.

My ex-husband, Michael, was excellent at playing the other mind-twister game, which I call **the "Blame Game."** After I questioned him for the first time about his sexuality two years into our marriage, he used this as an opening to play this game as his new weapon of mental torture. This is where he would come closest to revealing the truth by throwing in my face, "If I were gay, who could blame me? After all, you are always making too many sexual demands... complaining about something... gaining weight... acting jealous... being possessive... much too demanding.... all consuming... and the list went on. Then he would end the conversation with the words I desperately wanted and needed to hear—*"It's a wonder that I'm not gay."* Whew, what a relief. I was a failure as a wife, but at least not failure enough to make him gay.

A young woman who visits my on-line support sessions on Thursday evenings recently told us that on an intellectual level she knows she didn't make her husband gay, but emotionally she still feels that she is responsible. I often hear this in the beginning of a marriage separation. During the early stages of disclosure, it is easy to believe that we are somehow at fault for our husband's decision to enter the gay world. Even when we can accept the news, we still can't grasp all of the implications. We can't figure out how our husbands were "straight enough" to marry us, make love to us (even if it wasn't frequently or passionately), have children with us, have married lives with us but chuck it all for sex with a man. When we pass through the denial stage and accept that our husbands are gay, we still have a difficult time believing that it wasn't something we did that drove them over the borderline and into the twilight zone of homosexuality.

What takes time for us to fully comprehend is that we had no part whatsoever in our husbands' homosexuality. This was who they were long before we ever knew them. Some of them knew it and fought it hoping that marriage to a woman would miraculously make them straight. It can't...and it didn't. Others claim they honestly didn't know it because it didn't surface until years later.

But even the late bloomers almost always felt that something was not quite right—they just didn't think it was a sexual thing.

Playing the "If Only Game" is a very natural part of self-questioning that all of us initially go through. The problem is that some of us keep playing, sometimes for months and even for years. This is a dangerous game if played for too long because it indicates that you have not been able to put things into perspective. It also stops you from moving ahead and trying to rebuild your life. Prolonged questioning of your failures in the marriage serves no purpose at all. If you failed at the marriage, it's because you were in a no-win situation. You were set up for failure, not for success. Success was not an option.

If you had been in a marriage with an emotionally healthy straight man, all of your efforts of being a supportive and loving wife would have been appreciated and in fact, cherished. So don't use your marriage with a gay husband as a map for your future relationships. If you try again with a straight man, you'll see how different and better it can be. .

February 2002

HAPPY VALENTINE'S DAY--NOT

In the past, I have written about the difficulty that straight wives have during the holiday season. It is not uncommon for depression to set in somewhere around Thanksgiving and continue right through the New Year. During that six-week period, there are three holidays that revolve around family happiness and unity, something most of us are missing.

While we get caught up in the preparation for these holidays, we can't help but to feel an emotional letdown when they actually take place. We know what they represent, and yet, we never feel the wonder and joy of what the holidays represent that others are feeling. We go through the motions waiting for the emotional impact to kick in, but when it doesn't, that's when the depression sets in.

And now, just as we start to get back to our "normal" existence state of mind to cope in our relationships, we are once again brought down by the most hurtful holiday of all—Valentine's Day. This is the day that exemplifies love and romance. It's hearts and flowers all the way. It's the day that symbolizes what being in love is all about. It's a day where two people who love each other take the time to stop and think about that love and to remember how it feels to be "in love" even if some of the passion has faded through the years.

If you are the wife of a gay man, this is a day that really hurts. This day, more so than all of the other holidays, is a slap of reality about your marriage. You see, on the other holidays you can cover yourself with a veil of illusion because they are family holidays. Whatever you are lacking in your marriage can be compensated for through your children and other family members. But Valentine's Day is different. It's about the two of you. And no matter how you justify it by thinking it's a day of love in general, it's not. Yes, you can buy Valentine's Day cards for your son or daughter, mother and father, co-workers and friends to try to make it better. But there's really no escaping what it really is—a holiday for lovers.

The reason why this holiday in so painful is because it is upfront and personal and right in your face. No matter how you try to avoid dealing with the reality of living with a gay husband on a day-to-day basis and lull yourself into a false sense of security, Valentine's Day reminds you of the lie you are living with the man whom you fell in love with and married in good faith. It's a reminder of everything that you were supposed to have but were cheated from having. And the man who robbed you of your dreams is still lying in bed next to you. Each morning when you wake up with him next to you, it's one more day of living a lie.

Now the lie wasn't your lie to start with—it's his lie. But it has become your lie because you're living it with him. You're going through the motions of what marriage is supposed to be, but it's falling way short of what your intentions were when you made that commitment at the altar Your husband, who promised to love and cherish you through sickness and health 'til death do you part, never mentioned that he would never be able to love you the way you needed to be loved. In fairness, maybe he didn't know that he wouldn't be able to do it. No doubt, he was hoping that he could pull it off. And I'll even go so far as to say that maybe he didn't come to terms with the fact that he was gay on that life-changing day. But in almost all cases he knew he was having conflicting feelings. He knew something was off even if he couldn't figure out that it was homosexuality.

Even when I speak to gay men who tell me that they honestly didn't believe that they were gay, or hadn't acted on those impulses prior to marriage, they still knew looking or thinking about men sexually aroused them. And even if they still couldn't come to terms with that, they knew when they stopped making love to you early in the marriage that they were not attracted to you because you were a woman. But they kept quiet because they were afraid if they told you their secret, you may blow it for them. You might pull away their security blanket leaving them vulnerable and feeling naked. It wasn't always an easy choice for them to keep lying to you, but it was easier than telling the truth.

So to those of you who are living in one of the many situations that bring us all together under this umbrella of commonality, let me personally wish you a Happy **Future** Valentine's Day. Believe me, it can happen to you just like it happened to me. This is a day I celebrate in a big way. It's a day that makes me happy because I have a man whom I am in love with. He makes my heart flutter and my knees still get shaky when we touch—and that's after eight years. I don't say that to brag, but rather to let you know how life was meant to be. You were meant to have a man who can love you and make love to you. You were meant to meet someone who would cherish you and treat you as if you were the most important part of his life. The fact that you were sidetracked doesn't mean that you are doomed forever. It is never too late to find the happiness you are seeking as long as you don't give up hope. And even if you don't want to think about falling in love, at least think about not living in an abusive situation. Work on loving yourself enough to move away from a man who is not your soul mate but who is destroying your soul instead, one layer at a time.

Go out and buy yourself a giant box of chocolates. Enjoy each one of them as you remember how sweet life is supposed to be and how wonderful it will be once you remove yourself from a disastrous situation.

April 2002

LOW SELF-ESTEEM ISSUE

I can never talk enough about the issue of self-esteem. When I reflect back now, at the age of 50, I can honestly say that I have spent a lifetime building up my own self-esteem. I can trace this back to my early childhood days when I was always the "chubby" girl. Eventually I transitioned from being a chunky teenager to being an obese adult. I have spent my adult years being fat. There have only been short periods of perhaps several years from time to time when I was heavy instead of obese.

When I met my gay husband, I was physically at the best point of my adult life. I had lost over 100 pounds and I was feeling and looking good. My self-esteem and confidence was at a new height. I was NOT desperate when I met him, so I can't use that as an excuse of why I married a gay man. Like almost all of us, I honestly did not know that he was gay. It's that simple. He made sure to let me know that he wasn't by yelling up a storm when I mentioned a friend of mine suspected that he may be "bisexual." I remember that feeling of total relief when he stood up in the middle of the restaurant and nearly turned the table over in sheer anger. Ah, the man was protesting—and it couldn't be nearly enough--forget too much.

Why would I even think he was gay? He was tall, athletic, very handsome and extremely charming. We had sex in those early days. It wasn't the best sex, but it wasn't that bad either. I had worse in the previous years, and I believe that all of them weren't gay.

My ex-husband married me because he loved me and wanted to have all of the things that straight men had. And in his mind, at that time, he was NOT gay. Yes, he had gay sex. Yes, he had a string of sexual encounters with men before we married. But in his mind, he believed that he was straight because there was no emotional commitment to these men. He enjoyed women and dated his fair share of them. And he believed that sexually he could pull it off as long as he loved someone enough. Through the years, I have come to terms with the fact that most of these gay men really don't believe in their hearts that they are gay when they marry us. They can have gay sex galore, but they are not gay in their minds. They don't even view themselves as Bisexual, just straight men dabbling with same sex encounters. Go figure.

Getting back on track here, I married a man who was mentally abusive to me. Not all gay husbands take this route, but many of them do. They are frustrated with life because they are living a lie, and the one they lash out at is the one responsible for living this lie in their minds—namely, us. Yes, I know it makes no sense at all, but that's just the way it is. Even though my self-esteem was quite high when I got married, it didn't take long for it to get battered back into oblivion within a relatively short amount of time. I was on a temporary high when I met my husband. I was feeling good about myself for the first time in my 28 years of life. I had not even had two solid years of good feelings about myself before this marriage. That means that I had numerous years of personal insecurity, loneliness, poor self-image, and peer-inflicted pain scars from adolescence that carried over into adulthood.

I was the girl who was picked last to be on whatever sports team that gym class played on any given day. I lacked the motor coordination to be an effective sportswoman, and my excess weight slowed down my athletic abilities. It was pretty heartbreaking and humiliating knowing that you would always be the last or almost last person picked. I was the girl who never got asked to dances or proms. I was the girl who didn't have dates on the weekend because the guys I wanted didn't want me. They wanted the pretty cheerleaders or the girls who radiated confidence. I was the girl who fell in love so often but always had her heart broken time after time when some girl who was prettier, thinner, or more graceful crossed my path. Ultimately, I was the girl who got left out. There were so many of us when I was growing up, but that didn't make me feel any better. I wanted so badly to be someone worth loving, but that didn't seem within my reach.

For that reason, I made poor choices in relationships from early in the game. I just wanted to be wanted to badly, that I was willing to "settle" for guys, later men, who were not worthy of having a relationship with anyone. They were men who had value systems that were different than mine, but yet, my desperation kept me moving in their direction because they seemed more obtainable.

In my mid-twenties, I was nearly 270 pounds and at five feet tall, I wasn't long for the world. I began to care about living after having extensive chest pains, and started to lose weight. First I lost it in a healthy manner; then I developed an eating disorder when the healthy way just stopped working very well. Within 18 months, I lost approximately 130 pounds so I was feeling quite good about myself. I was never thin, but I was looking good, feeling good, and doing quite well in life. I was very vain at that point, and that was fine too. It was time for me to finally feel good about myself. Professionally, I was where I wanted to be, and personally, I was testing out the waters and looking for the right somebody to love.

Maybe if I had married a wonderful supportive man, my self-esteem building process would have continued on an upward trend. But instead, I found a man who was down right cruel who used to find great pleasure in knocking me down whenever I dared to stand up to question any of his unusual behaviors. This was his way of fighting back. My ex wasn't really a bad man, he was just a sad man. He was sad because his life was falling apart being married to me. He was lying all over the place to cover his tracks, and every time I would uncover just one little crack, he became so angry. He was trying to tie that web of lies together but I seemed to be untangling them faster than he could tie them.

Rather than accept responsibility for his misactions, my ex would yell and scream about my inadequacies. He would magnify every molehill into a mountain when it came to my imperfections, making me believe that I was the awkward, gawky, overweight teenager all over again. I didn't have enough "self-confidence" time accumulated to make me believe differently. After a while, I bought into all of the lies that my husband kept telling me about me as he shredded away the few good years of feeling good and reverted me back to my original form of feeling inadequate.

And so once again, I found my comfort in food and started putting back my weight, one pound at a time. When I became pregnant, I looked at it as a license to eat all I wanted because the weight would come off after the baby was born. That's what people kept telling me. I did gain 70 pounds during those months feasting on Baskin Robbins ice cream daily by the gallon. When my premature daughter was born and weighed less than five pounds, that's what came off my body. And although in time I was able to take off half that amount gained, I regained it when I was pregnant with my son. I was once again a fat woman.

When my husband told me that he couldn't make love to me because I was too fat, well, that seemed reasonable to me. At that point, I didn't think much of myself so why would I expect a man to think much of me? It sounded so logical and made so much sense.

I say this first of all because I receive letters from so many women who write to me and tell me that they are 20, 40, 60, 80, or 100 pounds overweight. They didn't start out that way in their marriage for the most part, but ended up that way due to frustration. Some of them had childhoods like mine where weight was a factor, but many of them never had a weight problem until during the marriage. They usually throw into their letters that marriage caused them to overeat because there was nothing else giving them much satisfaction on the home front. And as they gained weight,

I am sure that their husbands secretly cheered on the weight gain because now they had a new reason to retreat in the bedroom—namely, fat. Now fat became the natural enemy and justification for lack of passion, as if there was ever much passion to start with. Like my husband told me shortly before we split up, "Who would ever want to sleep with someone who looked like you? Have you looked at yourself lately in a mirror? If I became gay, who could blame me?" OUCH, with all capital letters. There were lots of tears that flowed from my eyes after that conversation. My ex had a wonderful talent for destroying any residual good feelings I had left from days of old. There was nothing left by the time he was done with me except a sense of survival—to find a way to survive without him in my life.

When I first started my local support group, the first two women who joined were also fat. I will not cover up that word and make it into something that it's not. I don't use that word to be insulting, but rather to be honest. I don't need a bunch of "feel good" words about what I am. I feel good about myself now even if I am fat. It's amazing what a wonderful straight man can do for your sense of self-worth. My soul mate hasn't noticed the weight gain I've made over the eight plus years we've been together. He still thinks I'm beautiful and makes me feel that way about myself.

But, getting back to the point, I thought at first it must be a thing that women of weight encounter because my first two group members were big women. But after that, I was shocked to find how many thin women who were beautiful, attractive, and graceful women by society's standards were in the same situation. As many of you know from my book, I still have my theories on the prototype of woman that a gay man seeks out when he wants to get married. One of the prototypes is a woman with low self-esteem. There are so many of us and we are all such easy targets. However, what I learned is that self-esteem is often something that women have within themselves from what's going on inside, not outside.

I recently corresponded with a lovely woman who read my book last year. She thanked me for giving her the key to the problem in her life. She is an airline stewardess who is viewed by men as beautiful. And yet, after nine years with her hands-off husband, she felt as deflated as the rest of us. She has now moved on in her life and feels wonderful about it. I hear from many women just like this-- women who have never had self-esteem issues over their looks. Over this year alone, I have worked with three models, two in New York and one in California who certainly didn't have a problem with their physical appearance. And yet, all of their external physical beauty didn't help them feel beautiful inside. Within this same time frame, I have helped women who were doctors, lawyers, nurses, stockbrokers, professors at universities, a CEO in a Fortune 500 company, and a Broadway actress. Certainly they had accomplished enough in their professional lives to be admired by the masses for their intelligence and status. And yet, they felt just as horrible about themselves as I used to feel about myself. It seems as if having a gay husband is the great equalizer among women of all sizes, shapes, colors, professions, economic situations and societal boundaries.

I guess what I'm getting to is simply this. If the beautiful women who had high self-esteem throughout their lives can fall into this dark and lonely hole, what chance do women like me-- who by society's standards have imperfections creating emotional baggage--have? If a woman who held her head high all of her life can have hers chopped off the block, why would I expect mine not to be in the same pile only squashed down a little more?

I talk about this because women write to me constantly looking for excuses of why their gay husbands may have been turned off to them. They write about their torment of how hard they tried to be better wives by dieting which sometimes led to eating disorders, having breast implants, liposuction, plastic surgery, changes in hair color, and so many other things to try to physically change their husbands' desire for them. It's almost as if they are still apologizing or looking for reasons why they were at fault. And their pain becomes my pain. I hurt for every woman who has to spend one extra minute not feeling good about herself because she has failed with her gay husband.

In my last newsletter, I wrote about the long awaited conversation that I had with my ex-husband that brought closure to our misunderstandings. I think that these are the feelings that our gay husbands and ex-husbands have to know and understand. It's not just the superficial damage or the obvious problems that result from these mismarriages. It's the internal damage and scaring that they just don't have a clue about.

I can forgive any gay husband for being gay. That is not a conscientious decision, nor is marriage a calculated move of deceit to punish some loving woman. And I acknowledge how difficult it is for gay men to come to terms with their homosexuality during a marriage. However, what I can't forgive is the cruelty that they display to their wives while going through their own hardships. And even when they are able to be honest and move on in their lives, they somehow lack the understanding of what we are left to deal with. They feel we should just be able to "get over it" as if we can walk away from the damaging years unscathed. Well, we can't and we don't. And perhaps when they can recognize this and try to undo some of the damage that they caused, a better understanding will come about between wives and gay husbands or ex-husbands. There is great comfort in knowing that your gay man understands that the hurt goes much deeper than just superficial cutting. And when he can comprehend that and tell you that he is sorry for the internal damage he has done to you, then you will finally be able to start to heal—and even start to forgive.

December 2003

ACT 2: SCENE 3

Quite frequently, women write to me about their lack of viable skills when it comes to securing a job so they can gain financial independence. I always look for transferable skills that would be a good match such as caretaker, nurse, detective, etc. How did I miss the most obvious one, namely—**ACTRESS**?

Every holiday season, wives of gay men have to play their Oscar award-winning role of "Happy Wife" in front of crowds of hundreds. Of course, there is no golden statue at the end of the season like their movie counterparts, but no doubt, the performances are just as extraordinary. And the holiday season is not the yearly birthday, anniversary, or Easter. The **HOLIDAY SEASON** is a long stretch that starts at Thanksgiving and continues until Valentine's Day. Between those two points, we begin the family and love ordeal. Thanksgiving is the beginning, followed by Christmas, New Year's, and finally ending on Valentine's Day in February. We are so relieved to have the President's Birthday as a holiday in February because by then, all of our emotional horror of the holiday season is over. Imagine thinking that Washington and Lincoln can actually neutralize and balance out life because after three months of families celebrating family unity and love, we no longer have to cringe when we hear the word, "holiday." The *touchy-feely* ones are over, and once again, we have not been touched or felt, and in fact, most of us have been living with a Novocain kind of numbness so that we can protect ourselves from crying at any given moment because we are HURTING.

The Holiday Season is such a difficult time for straight wives because it is an up front in your face reminder of what life was supposed to be like but never became. Or if it was, it's over after years because homosexuality has joined into your previously happy union or what you were hoping would be your happy union. It's almost like having Scrooge find his way into your husband's body and head. When you want a display of affection and emotion, he's saying, "Bah, Humbug." To this I say, "Ho, ho, no, no more."

You see, even though you may be feeling the pain of this holiday season, it could be your last year to suffer this way. Believe it or not, you can make it your New Year's resolution to be **FREE** by next year. **Free** of the pressures and strain *of living a lie.* **Free** of the constant questioning of what can you do to make life better with a man who wants a man to make his life better. **Free** of the mental torture from the mind games your husband plays so well with you, trying to make you start believing that *you* are losing your mind and it's just *your* imagination running away *with you* while *he's running around with men.* **Free** of earning your professional detective license while snooping around in a relationship that is supposed to be based on honesty and truth. **Free** to go to bed at night and feel good about waking up in the morning. Why? Because waking up alone and having peace of mind is always better than waking up next to someone who really doesn't want to be with you and is making you miserable because he feels that you are "trapping" him.

You see, way beyond this being a holiday season of family and love, it is a holiday season of hope. A time to make resolutions that will help you become healthy and happy. Now I know people hate clichés, but this one really catches the essence of the holiday—namely, "**HOPE SPRINGS ETERNAL.**" This little ditty kind of coincides with my own personal philosophy; namely, each new day offers the opportunity of waking up and changing your life. I believe it. I actually did it, and I never look back and regret it. My marriage was doomed. I could have spent 10, 15, or 25 more years of wasting my life with a man who could only make me miserable. But a little bird in my head that became a choir of canaries singing to me, "Don't Do It." Don't give up one more year of precious time to a debilitating situation."

April 2005

THE ISSUE OF COMMUNICATION

The most important part of any relationship is communication. This seems to be something that is sorely lacking in straight/gay marriages namely because they are built on lies and deception. Of course, this is not to say that it isn't missing in other kinds of relationships, regardless of sexuality issues, but it is even more so for ours. It's bad enough when we read about straight relationships and the lack of communication because women are from Venus and men are from Mars as the saying goes. But in our marriages, women are from Venus and men are from the Twilight Zone.

I always say that for the most part, straight wives married to gay men are far above the standards of wifedom. You see, women married to straight men have a fighting chance of pleasing their husbands just based on who they are. But we can never please our husbands because of who we aren't—namely men. But that doesn't stop us from trying harder and harder to put that round peg into a square hole, does it? And it never ceases to amaze me how so many of us just can't cry "uncle" and walk away from a no-win situation. We keep trying while we keep crying to figure out where we are going wrong long after we suspect or know the truth. Go figure.

It also saddens me to talk to women who just can't get it. Even when they are faced with the truth, they keep trying even harder to be the perfect wife as if perfection will turn around the gene pool. And I can say that it's not always their fault. Often it is the fault of the "confused" gay husband who just can't let go of the straight world even when he is not confused over what stimulates his sexual organ. Again, go figure.

Excuse me from digressing from my original thought of communication. I have recently revisited a painful part of my past. You see, even when the years have passed, as in my case, and the marriage is long over, the scars still remain. In spite of all of my expertise and counseling skills in relationship issues, I still have to be my own best student. And though it pains me to have to discuss my weaknesses in a forum read by thousands of people, I am a great believer in people learning from each other. So I will proceed to talk about this with you.

One of the areas of self-improvement I work on constantly is self-esteem. This is a definite tie to my ability to communicate in a healthy way in my relationship with my soul mate, which will soon reach the ten-and-a-half year mark. I have found a man who truly loves me more than I could have imagined. And yet, I still have fears that if I ask for some additional emotional support when I need it, I will be rejected. This angers me because it is so typical of behavior by someone who feels she is unworthy, which I do not. So why do I have to keep trying so hard?

My years with my gay husband trained me to be an excellent partner for any man. I am fully seasoned as far as working my hardest to make someone love me like all of you are. And to be honest, I've put everything I have into this present relationship. I work hard to keep it exciting and new after all of these years. We're middle-aged, but we feel like we're young and in-love. Our relationship is solid. I trust this man with my life. It took years of working at it to get it this way. We have both learned to compromise. He works hard to meet my emotional needs because to me, that's an important part of a relationship.

Well, to get to the point, several months ago, my soul mate didn't meet my expectations concerning something that was very important to me. I was hurt and angry. It was something simple that required very little effort, and yet it was very significant to me. He blew it and he knew it. He knew it instinctively and also because I did tell him. I honestly think he felt worse than I did because the last thing he ever wants to do is hurt me. In the following two days, he tried his best to make up for it by buying me flowers and cards that said emotional things. And I acted like I forgave him even though in my heart, I was still hurting.

So life went on and all was well—or so I thought. But over the days and weeks that followed, something was amuck—with me, not him. I didn't worry about it because I am pre-menopausal and expect to feel highs and lows. But the feelings I had were neither high nor low. There was a slow but gentle decline in my feelings for my soul mate. I went through the motions, but I wasn't feeling them. My soul mate knew something was off, but I kept saying it was everything *but what* it was.

Although I made excuses for why this was happening, I was unable to discover the real reason until weeks later. As I started to see that nothing was improving and it started impacting on our intimacy, I realized that there really was a problem that I needed to work on. I did some mental backtracking to the time when my feelings started to shift, and voila—I finally figured it out. It all led back to the time when he screwed up weeks before. And although he tried his best to patch it up with words of regret and flowers, I hadn't inwardly resolved the hurt.

I analyzed why I buried the hurt and it all comes back to the same thing--lack of self-esteem. Lack of feeling worthy enough to express my true feelings for fear he will back away or think that I am "nagging" or "suffocating" him. My gay ex-husband had me very conditioned not to ask for what he didn't want to give me. It always started a fight and I always lost because he had better verbal damaging skills than I had. In fact, all these years later, he still knows how to trigger those buried feelings of inadequacy whenever we have an argument. He can shout me down and shut me up because I don't like fighting on such a low level. I find it degrading.

My soul mate is not my ex-husband. He is kind and gentle, caring and giving. If I am upset about something, he takes it to heart. He has worked hard to change so he can meet my emotional needs. And 98 percent of the time, he does. It's the two percent of the time that always gets to me. And most times, I let it slide because no one is perfect and I know he has tried so hard to make me feel good about myself and about us. But this one time was something of great importance to me, and the usual "I'm sorry" just didn't cut it.

Once I recognized where the problem stemmed from, I sat down with him and said we need to talk because I finally understood what the problem was. And guess what? He didn't laugh at me or blow me off. He wasn't annoyed or angry. He listened and accepted my feelings, acknowledging that the hurt was deeper than we both realized. All was well again after that conversation. It was like a dark cloud being chased away and replaced by a lovely day.

It taught me a lesson, which is why I am sharing this with you. Through the years that our feelings are ignored or scowled at, we become conditioned not to ask because we would not receive. This behavior is easy to carry into our new relationships because we are still trying hard to please our new partners, subconsciously feeling that we failed with our gay ones. Every time we can't express our feelings fearing rejection, we are giving in to the horrors of our past marriages. Not being able to assert yourself in a relationship only continues to build on your feelings of inadequacy even when you are sure that they are dead and buried. It doesn't take much to revive them no matter how much you think you've left them behind.

Unless you internally believe that you are deserving of more, you will always settle for less. This is why I tell women who are leaving marriages with their gay husbands to wait before they jump into a new relationship with a man. You need time to relearn who you are and to work on the issues that can haunt you forever if you don't face them. Coming out of relationships with there is a lack of trust, intimacy, self and sexual esteem, and communication takes time. If you don't give yourself time to repair, chances are you will jump into the wrong relationship, or take a potentially good relationship and destroy it all on your own.

I have seen women who have met good men but destroyed the relationship because they haven't resolved their own issues with their gay husbands. They transfer them into their new relationships and disaster occurs. We allow our feelings of inadequacy and mistrust to surface anytime there is a problem, rather than allowing ourselves to rationally work it out. That's why we all need time and breathing space after our marriages to regroup and regenerate.

Now, this is not to say that you have to stay home and become a hermit like I did for many years. You can go out and have fun—and practice for your soul mate. But before you get in the relationship mode, make sure you work out kinks from your marriage. If you don't, you are setting yourself up for a big fall. You may choose the wrong partner because you still haven't restored your own sense of self-esteem. And one thing I've learned—no one can make you feel better about yourself except you. Only then can you find long-term happiness and fulfillment.

The most important thing to work on is overcoming your fear of asking for something that is important to you for fear of being rejected. We've tiptoed around our gay husbands not feeling worthy because they could never love us the way we needed to be loved. In a new relationship, stand up for yourself and don't be afraid to ask for what you want. That's how communication in healthy relationships works. Don't allow your insecurities of the past overtake your happiness in the future.

ABOUT THE AUTHOR

Bonnie Kaye, M. Ed., author of **The Gay Husband Checklist for Women Who Wonder**, is internationally recognized as a counseling expert in the field of straight/gay marriages. Since 1984, she has counseled over 35,000 women who discovered their husbands are gay. She has also worked with hundreds of gay men helping them to come out to their wives.

Kaye began her counseling after the demise of her own painful marriage to a gay man in 1982. Her books, support groups, and monthly newsletters have helped these women understand the dynamics of marriage to a gay man. Kaye's website at **www.Gayhusbands.com** offers information to get people connected.

Kaye received her Masters Degree in Counseling from Antioch University in 1986. She has appeared on international, national, and local television and radio to explain how this phenomenon happens and the damage it does to a marriage. She also consults for major national television talk shows and news shows about this subject. Kaye runs an online support group three times weekly to lend support to women during and after their marriages.

Kaye's other books include: *Doomed Grooms: Gay Husbands of Straight Wives; ManReaders: A Woman's Guide to Dysfunctional Men; Straight Wives: Shattered Lives;* and *How I Made My Husband Gay: Myths About Straight Wives.* **The Gay Husband Checklist for Women Who Wonder** is an updated version of her first book previously titled *Is He Straight? A Checklist for Women Who Wonder.*

Bonnie Kaye can be reached at **Bonkaye@aol.com**. She is available for private counseling sessions by telephone or email.

CPSIA information can be obtained at www.ICGtesting.com
Printed in the USA
BVOW04s1125110315

391214BV00001B/293/P